UFO's, ET's and paran

CW00351090

Synopsis

This is the story of genuine experiences of the Supernatural including ghosts, UFO's, alien abduction, MIB's, Pre-Cognition and metaphysical encounters throughout my life and the conclusions I have come to in an attempt to answer the questions that many have regarding these subjects that are avoided by science, but experienced by myself as true. I go on a journey of discovery travelling the Far East and even becoming a Buddhist monk, until I draw some conclusions weaving the experiences together to try to come to some understanding of what it all means.

Published by *TJ Owen*

Copyright © 2011 *TJ Owen*

With special thanks to Nick Redfern for advice and encouragement and to my parents who brought me into this world. To my oldest friend Neil Blakiston, Eduardo Novo (Bhikkhu Dhammiko). Ajahn Sumedo and Ajahn Nyanarato for their teaching, training and support. All Monks and Nuns and Spiritual beacons for being lights in the world and anyone I have not mentioned.

Also thanks to all the people whose work I have used and referenced in the making of this book including; Trevor J Constable, Albert Bender, William G Gilroy, P D Ouspensky, Eknath Easwaran, Neil Arnold, Emma Cooper, Christopher reeve and George Knapp.

T J Owen

Contents

1.Flying machines, birds of prey and CE 1-4

The first memory I have of something strange and interesting in the sky was when walking was just about possible. I was in the living room of my house with my mother, when a very loud noise could be heard and a shadow came over the room like an eclipse of the sun. What was that? I thought, I must go to see! As I struggled to my feet and made my way to the conservatory to see what could have possibly caused such a commotion, I was never to find out, as it was long gone by the time I got to the doorway. Blast! .. I was too slow was my thoughts, but it was something that stirred a great feeling inside, of adventure and curiosity, and I somehow knew it was of great importance.

Let us first establish what is meant by CE 1- 4 before we continue, below from Wikipedia is a rundown of the scale:

In ufology, a *close encounter* is an event in which a person witnesses an unidentified flying object. This terminology and the system of classification behind it was started by astronomer and UFO researcher J. Allen Hynek, and was first suggested in his 1972 book *The UFO Experience: A Scientific Inquiry.* He introduced the first three kinds of encounters; more sub-types of close encounters were later added by others, but these additional categories are not universally accepted by UFO researchers, mainly because they depart from the scientific rigor that Hynek aimed to bring to ufology.

Sightings more than 500 feet (160 m) from the witness are classified as "Daylight Discs," "Nocturnal Lights," or "Radar/Visual Reports." Sightings within about 500 feet are sub classified as various types of "close encounter." Hynek and others argued a claimed close encounter must occur within about 500 feet to greatly reduce or eliminate the possibility of misidentifying conventional aircraft or other known phenomena.

Hynek's scale achieved cachet with the general public when it informed elements of the 1977 film *Close Encounters of the Third Kind,* which is named after the third level of the scale. Posters for the film recited the three levels of the scale, and Hynek himself makes a cameo appearance near the end of the film.

Hyneks Scale:

First

A sighting of one or more unidentified flying objects:

- Flying saucers
- Odd lights
- Aerial objects that are not attributable to known human technology

Second

An observation of a UFO, and associated physical effects from the UFO, including:

- Heat or radiation
- Damage to terrain
- Crop Circles
- Human paralysis (Catalepsy)
- Frightened animals
- Interference with engines or TV or radio reception.
- Lost Time: a gap in one's memory associated with a UFO encounter.

Third

An observation of what Hynek termed "animate beings" observed in association with a UFO sighting. Hynek deliberately chose the somewhat vague term "animate beings" to describe beings associated with UFOs without making any unfounded assumptions regarding the beings' origins or nature. Hynek did not necessarily regard these beings as "extraterrestrials" or "aliens." Additionally, Hynek further expressed discomfort with such reports, but felt a scientific obligation to include them, at the very least because they represented a sizable minority of claimed UFO encounters.

Fourth

A human is abducted by a UFO or its occupants. This type was not included in Hynek's original close encounters scale.

Jacques Vallee, Hynek's erstwhile associate, argued that a CE4 should be described as "cases when witnesses experienced a transformation of their sense of reality," so as to also include non-abduction cases where absurd, hallucinatory or dreamlike events are associated with UFO encounters.

Fifth

Named by Steven M. Greer's CSETI group, these purported encounters are joint, bilateral contact events produced through the conscious, voluntary and proactive human-initiated or cooperative communication with extraterrestrial intelligence. This is very similar to some "contactees" of the 1950s who claimed regular communication with benevolent aliens.

While the nature of this bilateral communication is generally claimed to be telepathic, the experiencers in this group (as defined by CSETI) generally do not claim to be psychic if they should happen to think of themselves as contactees (in the strictest sense of the meaning of that terminology), insofar as contact, at least initially, is unilateral communication coming from the otherworldly intelligence to its subjects. Contrary to popular belief, not all experiencers in this group necessarily equate their communiqué as being with aliens.

Sixth

On Michael Naisbitt's website, a sixth proposed CE scenario is described as UFO incidents that cause direct injury or death. This category was not included in Hynek's scale, and is furthermore redundant: a CE2 in Hynek's scale specifically included UFO encounters that leave direct physical evidence of *any* kind.

Seventh

The Black Vault Encyclopedia Project proposes a Close Encounter of the Seventh Kind as mating between a human being and extraterrestrial that produces a human-alien hybridization, usually called a Star Child. This concept is similar to ideas promoted by ancient astronauts theorists like Erich von Däniken, Zecharia Sitchin and Robert K.G. Temple, in that extraterrestrials interacted with, perhaps interbred with and influenced ancient human beings in the past.

This concept of CE7 is at odds with Hynek's original concepts, however. Hynek's CE3 specifically avoided describing UFO occupants as "aliens" or "extraterrestrials," contending that there was not enough evidence to determine if beings associated with UFOs had an objective physical reality, let alone to confirm their origins or motives.

With that said we move forwards to the year 1977. I was 12 years old and lived in the countryside; a friend had asked me to do his early morning paper round for him whilst he was on holiday for a week. You had to be 13 yrs old to do an early morning paper round, but as there was no-one else to do it in the quiet village the distributors allowed me to do it. One of these mornings I was cycling down Bailes lane, a dead end road with common land at the end which went for miles toward the nearest town Guildford and had a couple of farms which were accessible by tracks from the end of the lane onto the common land. As I was cycling past the fields on the way to the end I felt something on my shoulder. I turned to look and there looking straight at me was a bird, a bird of prey no less, it looked like a Buzzard. I had the feeling that it was saying 'hello' to me. I said hello back in my mind and it then took off and flew away. That was a very strange occurrence, It left me with a nice feeling, but not as strange or nice as what was about to confront me.

I turned the corner and was pedalling up a slight incline towards the end of the lane when ahead and to the right under the dark heavily laden cloud cover was a bright light. It was elliptical in shape and had very defined edges despite the light emanating from it being extremely bright, brighter than any normal light (*close encounter of the first kind*). It was completely silent, and moving in a slow South Easterly direction towards Guildford. The idea of space and its inhabitants was of interest to me, I watched 'Dr Who' and 'UFO' and 'space 1999' with glee and excitement. I would imagine a spaceship coming down and the jolly spacemen inviting me aboard to see the ship and maybe even take me for a trip aboard.

But on seeing this ship of light in front of me, I stopped pedaling and became motionless. In fact I found that I was extremely scared and I was now unable to move any of my limbs (*Close encounter of the second kind – Human Paralysis or catalepsy*). I wanted to turn around and cycle home as fast as possible to get away, but I was frozen, like a rabbit caught in the headlights of a car. The ship slowly passed across in front of me, silently, it was perhaps 50 to 100 foot across, I wasn't sure as I couldn't judge the distance, maybe bigger? My head and eyes moved with the craft as it went across the horizon, it was involuntary movement as the only thing I really wanted to move was my legs in furious pedalling! All the time as I could see the craft, in my head I was saying a mantra "Don't come near me, don't come near me, don't come near me, Go away, go away, go away" over and over again I would be saying this in my head as the ship passed silently in front of me. Now it was off to the left of me and the clouds had a few breaks in them, the craft went behind a cloud, came out, went behind another cloud, came out, went behind another cloud .. this time it didn't come out. After a few seconds when I was sure that it had gone and didn't return, full use of my limbs became restored and I was able to cycle back home in a rush.

Back home, I rushed into the house and told my mother what I had seen. One of my sisters was there and heard everything, but didn't believe a word, she said to my mother "oh he just doesn't want to do the paper round and is trying to get out of doing it". Nothing could be further from the truth. I was too frightened to go back out again and my mother helped with the paper round that day. So now I learned to keep quiet, not to mention things of that nature to anyone as people didn't believe. But I was shown something extraordinary that day, that the world was a place where things were possible, things that even science and education say don't exist. But there it was, plain as day flying through the sky, so what else is possible? What else really exists?

In UFO lore sometimes people have 'screen memories' either implanted or their minds create a false memory to cover what they actually saw, as the reality is too much for the conscious mind to cope with. It seems popular for people to have dreamt about or remember seeing an owl when in fact it was an alien visitation. In this case I saw a bird of prey that landed on my shoulder, a very unlikely scenario in reality, it was in fact more likely to be a cover memory for something far more interesting (*close encounter of the third and fourth kind*).

My interest in UFO's was now cemented, and I fervently looked for all explanations for the existence of UFO's. Not because I thought they were great and fascinating, but because I wanted to **disprove** my experience, that I could put the thought in my head that they weren't real and what I saw was a phenomenon of nature. Perhaps some rare but real phenomena that was *not* visiting advanced cultures from another place, because I couldn't sleep well at night anymore, not knowing what was out there in the night. But after a long search, I found I could not disprove the experience. There was lots of good reasons put forward by intelligent people why they couldn't be here, but the reality of experience showed them to be wrong. There was no easy sleeping in bed at night after all.

Drawing of my 1977 sighting of a UFO

Ordinance survey map showing where I was on the 1977 sighting marked by the pin. The UFO was following the hog's back towards Guildford to the right of the map.

2.MEN IN BLACK

In UFO lore there are these people called "The Men in Black" (M.I.B.) who come around to UFO witness's homes and question and threaten the witness's to silence over their experience or sighting of the alleged UFO. Sometimes they arrive in pristine old black cars or arrive and disappear mysteriously. Often they seem not like Humans but more like aliens or some kind of Android, even using make-up and lipstick to hide their inhumanly looks.

We will start with a couple of reported interactions with M.I.B's to get a feeling of what they seem to be about:

Albert K Bender established what was one of the first UFO investigation groups called the International Flying Saucer bureau (IFSB) in Bridgeport, Connecticut, during 1952. The Bureau became so popular that it grew rapidly, and it eventually had centres all over the world. Members would investigate UFO reports locally and these were then often printed in their publication, entitled Space review.

The IFSB had appointed experts in the field of aeronautics, photography and astronomy by early 1953. They would evaluate and analyze the reports accumulated by the bureau and Gray Barker who had his own publication called the Saucerian was given the post of Chief investigator. This was a good time for the IFSB and the future looked rosy for the bureau, until in September 1953 three men in dark suits made an unannounced visit to the home of Albert K Bender and bought about the abrupt halt to all of his investigative UFO work. This was less than a month prior to the fourth quarter release of Space Review in which bender had promised to reveal information of great importance to its readers. Instead of this revealing information there was a statement about the *closing* of the IFSB along with two cryptic items:

"LATE BULLETIN. A source, which the IFSB considers very reliable, has informed us that the investigation of the flying saucer mystery and the. Solution is approaching its final stages. "This same source to whom we had preferred data, which had come into our possession, suggested that it was not the proper method and time to publish this data in Space Review." "LATE BULLETIN. A source, which the IFSB considers very reliable, has informed us that the investigation of the flying saucer mystery and the solution is approaching its final stages. "This same source to whom we had preferred data, which had come into our possession, suggested that it was not the proper method and time to publish this data in Space Review." The other item: "STATEMENT OF IMPORTANCE. The mystery of the flying saucers is no longer a mystery. The source is already known, but any information about this is being withheld by orders from a higher source. We would like to print the full story in Space Review, but because of the nature of the information we are very sorry that we have been advised in the negative. "We advise those engaged in saucer work to please be very cautious." So what actually happened to make such a turnaround for Bender, he was to keep quiet too scared to breath a word for many years until he decided to publish a book about his experiences: FLYING SAUCERS AND THE THREE MEN, in 1962. And as described here, they were definitely not human. This is how their first clear appearance is described:

"The room seemed to grow dark, yet I could still see. I noted three shadowy figures in the room. They floated about a foot off the floor. My temples throbbed and my body grew light. I had the feeling of being washed clean. The three figures became clearer. All of them were dressed in black clothes.

They looked like clergymen, but wore hats similar to Homburg style. The faces were not clearly discernible, for the hats partly hid and shaded them. Feelings of fear left me, as if some peculiar remedy had made my entire body   immune   to   fright.

The eyes of all three figures suddenly lit up like flashlight bulbs, and all these were focused upon me. They seemed to burn into my very soul as the pains   above   my   eyes   became   almost   unbearable.   "

FLYING SAUCERS AND THE THREE MEN (page 90) by Albert Bender,   1962

Here he gives us a clearer description when they appear to him in a more physical   form:

"Their clothing was made of a black material which reminded me of cloth used in the attire of clergymen. It was well pressed, appeared almost new. All the other apparel, such as ties, shirt, stockings, and shoes was also black.

Their faces were unpleasant to look at. Their eyes shone like tiny flashlight bulbs, and the teeth were pearly white, set in a very dark complexion. I could not see their hands, covered by black gloves. A bluish radiance enveloped their entire bodies, and I wondered if this was giving off the sulphuric   odor."

FLYING SAUCERS AND THE THREE MEN (page 106) by Albert Bender, 1962

13

What the three M.I.B.'s had told Bender was evidently the *solution* to the UFO mystery, but then ordered him to keep quiet and not to tell anyone or he would face going to prison. The whole episode and experience frightened bender so much he decided to finish his investigations and close down the bureau.

So lets look at another case of M.I.B.'s this time only one M.I.B on his own:

Peter Rojcewicz was researching his Ph.D. thesis in folklore, when he encountered a man in black. Like some other Men in Black reports, this one has been interpreted as having its origins not in physical reality, but in an altered state of consciousness.

One afternoon in November 1980, Rojcewicz was in the University of Pennsylvania library, seated near a large window at a table. "Without any sound to indicate that someone was approaching me from behind," said Rojcewicz, "I noticed from the corner of my eye what I supposed was a man's black pant leg. He was wearing rather worn black leather shoes."

A tall, slender man with deep-set eyes and a dark complexion stood by the table. After gazing out the window for a moment, the man sat near Rojcewicz. His suit was somewhat dingy and oversized, hanging loosely on his slim frame. With a slight "European" accent, the man asked Rojcewicz what he was doing; Rojcewicz replied that he was researching similarities between UFO accounts and earlier tales from various folklore traditions. A brief conversation about UFOs then ensued.

The man asked if Rojcewicz thought that UFOs were real. Rojcewicz replied that he was less interested in the physical reality of UFOs than he was in studying them from the perspective of a folklorist.

The man suddenly became angry, shouting, "Flying Saucers are the most important fact of the century, and you're not interested?" Rojcewicz feared that the man was a "lunatic" and tried to "calm him," after which the man became silent. The man then stood, placed his hand on Rojcewicz's shoulder and said something like, "Go well in your purpose."

Soon after Rojcewicz grew anxious and frightened as he became aware of how profoundly strange the brief encounter had been. "I got up," he wrote, "walked two steps in the direction he had left in, and returned to my seat. Then got up again, I was highly excited and walked around to the stacks at the reference desk and nobody was behind the desk. In fact, I could see no one at all in the library. I've gone to graduate school, and I've never been in a library when there wasn't somebody there! No one was even at the information desk across the room. I was close to panicking and went quickly back to my desk. I sat down and tried to calm myself. In about an hour I rose to leave the library. There were two librarians behind each of the two desks!"

So you can see they are highly strange beings who don't necessarily conform to normal reality or accepted modes of behavior. Now let's look at my own experience with M.I.B.'s:

I had not heard of the men in black, even though stories of them could be found perhaps in UFO literature, as I was not a reader of such things at 12 years old, I only knew of UFO's through the popular programmes on television. But never the less I was to be visited by these strange men in the dead of night, when I was asleep. They would not present themselves physically in my room (that I can remember anyway), but rather they would come into my dreams. I was not aware of their meaning for many years until I learned of the men in black and finally remembered my boyhood dreams.

What would happen is I would dream of these 2 men, they were featureless, they had no faces that I could remember, and they were dressed as business men, black trousers and jackets and ties, white shirts and black hats. They would always be after me and I would always be running away from them. The feeling they gave was not a normal one, but bizarrely had a sexual nature to it. I was quite confused about these dreams and wondered what they meant. One thing that became clear was that I was most certainly not homosexual, which was my fear for a while, as I'm sure you can understand. And so I put it down to just one of those things you go through when growing up, perhaps just strange feelings that is a part of adjusting to becoming an adult. Why would the men in black chase someone in their dreams, especially when the victim does not even know of the men in black? And indeed they never told me exactly why they were chasing me, or that I should never speak of my close encounter. The members of my family and society in general put that one firmly in place. The feeling of them being after me could be the most effective way of scaring a young boy? However it does show that these entities cannot just be physical, but are also of a psychic or ethereal nature. There are also M.I.B that appear to come from government agencies and are real people, but these are not connected to the more mysterious ones that I encountered in my opinion and maybe the government agencies are simply trying to copy the mode and behavior of the real M.I.B's as a cover for their own activities and investigations. As if someone said they were visited by the men in black, but it was in fact the government agencies people would not believe the story so easily or put it down to fabrication, thus covering the agencies activities.

3.DREAMS

I had a lot of interesting experiences related to dreams, The UFO experience seemed to have been a catalyst for a load of other experiences to unfold, or was it always going to be this way from the start?

I became interested in the waking and dreaming world, I pondered on how your consciousness went from waking consciousness to sleeping consciousness. How did you cross over, where was the point of no return, just how does it work? So I set about trying to find out. It's a practical experiment and not an easy one to complete. It basically comprises of watching yourself fall asleep and trying to notice at what point you go into sleep. I watched myself, and watching yourself falling asleep almost guarantees that you won't sleep, because it's a foreign concept to your mind.

Normally you let go and think of something nice and then drift away into sleep. So for a few nights I couldn't sleep at all, and then for a few nights eventually through sheer tiredness fell asleep without notice. But eventually I got the practice just right. When I was very tired and the mind really needed the sleep, I would notice that the dots of like white light that I could see on the back of my eyelids would begin to move around and form vague shapes. Then these shapes would become pictures and then as I got interested in the pictures I would follow them, and following these pictures took me into sleep. That's it! I exclaimed to myself, that's how it's done! You see pictures and get involved in them and follow them into sleep. Great but hang on what's going on now? Suddenly I realised that I was sleeping, but, was conscious of sleeping. I was aware of being in sleep. So I started to take advantage of this and tried to make happen in my dreams what I wanted. This is fantastic, a playground for the mind. Interesting as it was it made sleeping a whole lot of fun. I would go to my bedroom in the middle of the afternoon just so I could lay down and go into conscious sleep or as we know it 'Lucid dreaming'. One time I thought about space and the depths of the universe, I was interested in the size and breadth and so tried to imagine it in my mind. I thought of where I was lying on my bed and kind of 'zoomed' out like a telephoto lens that was on full zoom but now retracting back. So I zoomed out to see the village, then further to see the county from the air, ok.. now further to see the planet. Now it gets interesting to try and imagine the all the planets and the universe.. Then all of a sudden it was so black! And then a feeling came of standing on the edge of infinity. My breath was sucked away and I felt like I was on the edge of something so vast that I would be sucked in forever and never get out. This was my first spiritual experience, the feeling of infinity an experience rarely met, only by the most austere contemplatives in the depths of meditation. I wasn't ready for such an experience at such a young age, I pulled myself back into normal consciousness and took a deep breath ..

"wow, I'm not doing that again" .. not for many years yet anyway!

4.MOON

One strange dream I had was of the Moon, I was in the field adjoining my house running through the green grass, when I turned around to see the hedge that runs parallel to the track to my house. Instead of seeing just the sky above the hedge, I saw the moon, but not at the distance one usually equates with the moon, this time it was like the moon was almost touching the earth. The whole of the sky was filled with the upper half of the moon as if you were in a spacecraft and flying so close to the moon that it was all you could see. It was awe inspiring and breathtaking, why have such a dream, what could it mean? It would give me a lifelong interest in the moon and some other odd experiences with seeing the moon. I always wondered if in fact it was a memory of perhaps seeing the moon in exactly that way, perhaps aboard a spacecraft?

Another other odd experience with the moon was much later in life whilst I was in my early 40's. I was driving to work one morning, I started at 4am so was between 3.30 and 4.00am when the moon as I came towards Maidstone in Kent was nearly full and up to my left hand side, south eastwards. I noticed how beautiful it looked in the clear morning sky. The very next day I was driving again at the same time along the same road when I noticed the moon was off to my right, in a lower angle than the previous morning and in the south westerly direction? How was this possible? Surely I wasn't the only one to notice? Mind you there's hardly anyone about at that time of day, in the winter on a dark cold morning! Sometimes the moon can seem closer to the earth than at other times, and there is a strange atmospheric effect with magnification of things on the horizon and this could be why the moon seems closer sometimes when viewed on the horizon. But at other times it certainly seems larger than it does normally, does it move? Is it actually under the control of an intelligence? The feeling that the moon is more than a dead satellite comes to my mind often. There is interesting information pointing to the fact that I may be right:

There is evidence for the moon being a 'hollow object' it comes from the fact that when meteors strike the Moon, the latter rings like a bell. More specifically when the Apollo crew in November 20, 1969 released the lunar module, after returning to the orbiter, the module impact with the Moon caused their seismic equipment to register a continuous reverberation like a bell for more than an hour. The same effect occurred with Apollo 13's third stage which caused the Moon to ring for over three hours. Two Soviet scientists, Vasin and Shcherbokov, have spent much of their careers examining the facts compiled on lunar phenomena. Their conclusion is that the Moon is *artificial*, possibly a hollowed-out planet, and that it was steered from some distant region of the galaxy into a circular orbit around our planet (hence the extraordinary mystery of rock and Moon-dust age variations). They also claim that intellectual life has existed in the Moon for eons.

Also as NASA envisions it, astronauts will return to the moon within the next decade or so. These astronauts will build a permanent base and prepare for an historic undertaking that will send explorers to Mars. As Clive Neal, associate professor of civil engineering and geological sciences at the University of Notre Dame, envisions it, these same astronauts may be in for a shocking surprise.

Neal and a team of 15 other planetary geologists have reexamined data from seismometers placed by Apollo astronauts at lunar landing sites from 1969 to 1972. They found that instruments from Apollo missions 12, 14, 15 and 16 consistently radioed back seismic data to Earth until they were turned off in 1977 in a NASA cost-cutting measure.

19

"The moon is seismically active," Neal said. "When a quake occurs, the moon rings like a bell."

"Between 1972 and 1977, the Apollo seismic data detected 28 shallow quakes," Neal said. "A few of the shallow quakes registered up to 5.5 on the Richter scale. A magnitude 5 quake on Earth can move heavy furniture and crack plaster."

"The moon is a technology test bed for establishing such networks on Mars and beyond," he said.

(Source: University of Notre Dame, by William G. Gilroy)

5.NIGHTMARES

There was a downside to be able to have lucid dreaming at will, it means that virtually all dreams become lucid, even nightmares!

I had a particular nightmare that plagued me, it was always to do with a particularly evil doll. It was one of those ventriloquists dolls. It had black hair staring eyes and that wooden jaw that goes up and down, clack, clack, clack. This is well before the famous 'Chucky' horror films were ever conceived. I had seen a Dr Who episode with a doll controlled by the 'master' which scared me to death for some unknown reason. And another programme made some years later of an African doll with a spear that came alive, my fear may have been because of these aforementioned programmes. This ventriloquist doll would chase me through my dreams and sometimes have a monster friend who also joined in the chase. But there came a point when the nightmare would reach its ultimate climax.

In this particular nightmare the doll was on its own, and, as seems to be the case in these nightmares, they always were on familiar territory. I was running across the fields near to my home, running,

running away from the doll. I couldn't see the doll, but knew it was after me, that feeling of being chased again, that feeling of knowing something is after you. As I ran across the fields I saw the massive corrugated metal barn just outside and headed for it, I'll hide in there I thought, and ran straight inside. Where shall I hide?.. oh no.. I know it's coming, and now I've left myself in a dead end how will I get out?

Inside the barn was pitch black, no light at all, I felt my way deeper inside, right at the far end there was a metal stairway leading up to a platform. I ran up the stairway and onto the platform. It won't find me up here I thought. Wrong … I heard the 'clop' 'clop' 'clop' of those little wooden feet running across the cement floor of the barn.. My heart starts to beat faster.. and faster .. then all of a sudden .. 'Clang' .. the footfall of a wooden foot on a metal staircase. I can't see anything its pitch black … but I can hear the 'clang' 'clang' 'clang' 'clang' 'clang' of wood on metal as the doll is running up the metal staircase towards me. My heart is beating as fast as it ever has now. What can I do where can I go.. I can't stand it any longer, I want to escape .. so I thought "I know, I'll jump, throw myself down onto the concrete floor and with the bang of hitting the floor I will wake up, you never actually hit the bottom anyway you always wake up with a start". So I jumped, I had the sensation of falling.. and.. bang.. I hit the floor.. oh no, I'm still asleep .. what now? Then all of a sudden all I can hear is that noise of the doll running back down the metal staircase 'clang' 'clang' 'clang' 'clang' 'clang' 'clang'. I can't be any more scared, frightened to death I close my dream eyes and say to myself "wake up, wake up" but to no avail. Then all of a sudden "CHOMP" finally the doll has caught up with me and has taken hold of my leg and is now biting on my foot.

The fear is at maximum, I can't be any more scared than I already am, so I close my eyes tight as possible and say to myself.. "wake up, wake up" .. twice I do this, still with the doll chomping on my foot. Finally my eyes are actually opening in real life and I can see my bedroom. But wait.. what's that? The doll! It's there at the end of my bed, chomping on my foot through the duvet. I can't believe my eyes .. "I'm awake, but it's still here, it can't be?" .. so I furiously close my eyes tightly and say "wake up, he can't be there?" but he still is so I try again.. but the doll is still there, desperate and going crazy I try for a third time.. this time the doll is gone.

How can it be possible, it came into real life.. I saw it, it was there at the end of my bed. Ok so now lucid dreaming has taken a new turn, but not a good one. The line between waking and dreaming is blurring, what's real and what isn't? can you will something into being? Was it just my imagination? I certainly hoped so, but the feeling of that doll biting my foot seemed real enough.

There is a positive end to this nightmare story though. As again on another night I dreamed of this doll together with a monster friend of his chasing me through the garden of my house. I was running, because that's what I always did, then I realised I was running out of habit, I realised that the fear I had on our last meeting took fear to its limit. I actually had no fear left to feel. I stopped running, I turned around and watched as the doll ran towards me. Then I said "come on then" and as the doll reached me I kicked out, and kicked the doll over the garden hedge. Then I willed the doll to come back again, so that I could kick the doll to pieces, which I did. I never had another nightmare about the doll or his monster friends after that, I was free of them. But an even more important realisation was made. That fear itself has a limit, it has an actual limit, beyond which fear becomes pointless, and so it just ceases to exist. This also was a good insight into the nature of reality, what *is* real, reality is what the mind decides it's going to be. I saw the doll in my bedroom and felt its bite, it's presence, for those moments that is what reality was for me.

So you can shape your dreams with lucid dreaming, but there are limits and even though I tried to make the dreams exactly as I wanted, there was always the limit of what my mind let me do. For instance I decided to drive a smart silver sports car, fast down the road. But no matter how hard I pushed the accelerator it never seemed to go fast enough. And when I thought it would be a real bugger if I got a flat tyre … pshhhht, there it was, a flat tyre. So I never really had total control over the dreams, my mind. So is it also then possible to shape reality as I wanted it? Of course there would be limits, but perhaps reality is no different to the dream and can be shaped and manipulated by my will?

6.Remote Viewing

One of the things I enjoyed with Lucid dreaming, and even to this day is flying in my dreams and going to other places. I wondered if within my dreams I could actually go places and see them as they really were in reality. My in-built nosey nature wanted me to go and visit places and people in my dream state, so one day I decided to visit the house of a friend, and I decided to go in a rather unique way, through the Ariel of a television and look out at the occupants of the house through the television screen. So this I did, but as I looked out through the screen I saw the owners dog. Somehow the owners dog knew something was there and started to bark angrily at the screen, this had a strong effect on me and I felt the fear of the dog, which made my own hair stand up on end, and it made me back out of the house at a rapid speed and back to my own house whereupon I woke up and vowed never to do that again as I felt quite scared myself. I didn't know at the time but Remote viewing is something that was being developed by the US army at SRI

(Stanford research Institute), the remote viewers didn't sleep though but were in a kind of meditative state whereby they could go and *view* remote places for espionage reasons. (see penetration – the question of extraterrestrial and human telepathy by Ingo Swann)

7.Pre-cognitive Dreams

A developed dream world led to other experiences, I sometimes dreamt of my future life in allegorical terms. The path of my life is normally represented by pathways and tracks in the countryside. I saw who I believed was my future wife down one of these tracks. A lady shorter than me, all I could see was long black hair, her head drooped downwards so her face could not be seen. I passed her and thought 'oh she looks sad' and went back to talk to her, waking before the conversation started. Indeed my future wife was Asian with long black hear and of a small stature, and indeed after meeting I left, but went back and eventually married her. Another of these 'life' dreams involved me running down the tracks and across fields, trying to escape something unseen. I eventually hid behind a hedge thinking I was really well hidden, but the 'something' in pursuit knew exactly where I was and came straight to where I was hiding. What this represented is open to interpretation, but I was left with a feeling that there literally is 'Nowhere to hide' and that I can be found no matter what I did or where I went. I always associated this with an 'Alien' presence, the 'watchers' as I always thought of them.

One of my dreams was very exact, I was walking down a path near my home when I was a teenager, maybe 14yrs old, I had something in my hand that I looked at with a glance, but couldn't tell what it was. Then I looked up quickly and a bus came along the road, stopped at the bus stop not far in front of me and some people got out. Then the dream ended, I forgot all about the dream as it seemed inconsequential at the time. But one day maybe a few days or a week later an old friend was visiting, who was living in the US but came with some toys, one was a pair of 'walkie-talkies', which were not available as such in the UK at that time. So I was very proud to be having one as I walked along the road with my friend just behind. I looked down glancing admirably at the walkie-talkie, then all of sudden I recognised the moment. It was like the dream I had before. I looked up suddenly to see the bus, yes, there it was! Coming along the road just as I had seen, then it stopped and some people got off, all exactly the same as my dream. That was where the dream ended. I turned and shouted excitedly "I have seen this, in a dream, exactly this!" my friend looked a little taken aback, but actually accepted something must have happened by the excitement I was in. It may at first seem like nothing in particular, but it was the beginning of me trying to shut off the many experiences that were to keep pouring into my life. I thought about this incident during the following days and weeks, and realised that what I saw happened in my dream, through my own eyes, *exactly* as it had happened in reality. The same bus, the quickness I looked up (but only because I had seen it already, and in the dream I had *also* seen it already!) and all the cars, my friend, the way I held the walkie-talkie, the people on the bus.. *all* of them, destined to be there at exactly that time, in exactly those places, wearing the same clothes doing the same things. *How* could this be possible? Does that mean we have no choice? Are we all destined to do the things we do, and we can't change it? And again, something else that is supposedly *not possible*, but here it is, a reality, but denied by all those we look up to as the holders of truth, the governments, the Politian's, the education system and the all knowing scientists. Who *can* you trust, it seemed everyone was lying and at the same time denying the very experiences I was having. UFO's, aliens, seeing the future, scary monsters? Just what *is* possible? I eventually figured out there *must* be limits, after all I can't fit an elephant in my pocket, that's not possible, so there must be a limit, but to my young mind it was all getting too much, and I would eventually try to block it all out for many years, but not before I had some more strange experiences.

I had another 'path of life' dream, but this time I was in a building, following corridors and taking which direction I felt was best, when eventually I came across a booth to the left, in it was a young lady, it had a kind of cut out in the glass for speaking, rather like in modern banks. Just past it to the right was a room, which looked like a gymnasium of sorts. It was maybe 20ft square, and had a climbing frame to the right and to the left was like a viewing room, with glass panels so that people could see into the room, but the entrance to the viewing room came from outside the building, which feels rather like outside of life in a way. There was a door leading into the gym from the passageway I was in and on the far wall of the gym was a large archway maybe 10ft across which went into complete darkness. I was fascinated by this room and asked the lady what it was for. I also asked should I carry on or go into the room. She shrugged and said "up to you" and that was all she would say.

I couldn't resist it and entered the room. I looked around and looked through the windows to see people going about their business outside, which I found quite strange as there isn't normally anyone in these kinds of dreams except myself or people directly related to my life. It was definitely one of '*those*' kinds of dreams as it had a kind of realism and feel to it that was different to normal dreams. Then people started to enter the 'Viewing room' off to the left. It was all kind of irregular, I didn't recognise any of these people and I could see their faces quite clearly. They also had a very strange kind of look to them, they were emotionless and straight faced. They sauntered into the viewing room and just watched, silently.

So I looked at the climbing apparatus and thought "this is strange.

What's it for?" I climbed up a bit then got off again. Ok so now the dark exit to the back of the room was taking my attention and I started to walk towards it. As I neared the archway I noticed that the floor curved slightly to the left the other side of the archway and then went down quite steeply into the darkness below. As I went into the darkness I suddenly felt a bit scared, and then I didn't know how, but I *knew* that this was a representation of going down into my own mind, the darkness of the unknown part of my unconscious mind. I walked slowly and was feeling rather scared when all of a sudden I heard a noise, then I looked and something was coming up out of the darkness towards me. It wasn't small either! I saw some large legs and then decided that to turn and run for it was the best option. So I ran out of the tunnel and back into the gym, I saw the climbing frame and thought I should climb up it to get away and hopefully out of reach of the beast coming up.

I climbed the climbing fame and looked down in scared anticipation, and out of the darkness came the most enormous spider ever, itself maybe 7 or 8 feet across, and standing another 7 foot high. But there was something different about this spider, it had a head, a *human* head. It had the head of a female. The large half human half spider stopped and didn't even attempt to climb the frame after me, she just stopped and looked at me and said "you don't want to go down there, it's dangerous" it was more of a friendly warning than a threat, there was no malice or threatening behaviour from this being, then she wandered back through the archway and down into the darkness once more. I recovered from the experience reasonably quickly and felt that even though she seemed quite friendly, I didn't really want to come across her again. But there was an even bigger curiosity now with the dark recess of my mind, and I climbed down and stepped carefully back into the darkness of the descending tunnel. I paused momentarily in the darkness waiting for the steps of the large spider to return, ready to turn and run back to the climbing frame. But the spider did not return and with my heart pumping harder I stepped more into the darkness, what happened next is not known as the next thing I knew I was awake in the morning.

8. TIME

Time as shown by science is relative to the observer and here I experience time in an altogether different way to those around me.

I was in the garden of my family's house and playing with Neil a close friend of mine, when my sister came along with one of her friends. My sister decided to go inside a makeshift camp that was made around a climbing frame in the garden with her friend. So I decided this was an opportunity to annoy the girls by throwing a tennis ball into the air and getting it to drop inside the camp through a large hole in the roof. The desired effect was achieved and eventually the girls came storming out of the camp. An argument ensued and eventually my sister lost her temper and decided to throw the ball straight at my face. This is where things got really interesting, as she pulled her arm back in order to throw the ball all of a sudden everything seemed to stop. There was no sound, but all of the other of my senses seemed to be working. Then I realised that things had not stopped entirely, as I could see that her arm was slowly springing forwards in the motion of catapulting the ball towards me. Amazed and a bit shocked I slowly took in my surroundings, my eyes were moving at the same pace as everything else and I was aware of what was going on, but I was thinking in normal space-time. As far as my consciousness was concerned I was aware in normal space-time, but that all physical reality had slowed down to about 25 times slower than normal. It soon became apparent that I would have to do something about the ball that was about to come straight at me and so started to raise my right arm to try to block the oncoming ball, although it was still firmly in the grip of my sisters hand and had not yet left it. I could feel a kind of resistance of the arm against what I felt was the atmosphere, or could have been just the physical limits of possibility as I tried to raise the arm upwards. It was slow going, and I realised that there may not be enough time to get the arm in place. I again took notice of where the ball was and now it was beginning to leave the hand of my sister. I could tell that the two were not destined to meet as my arm was not going fast enough. I then had the strangest feeling that I could in fact break out of this slow motion mode, and go back to normal physical speed. So as my arm came up I thought, well, maybe if I suddenly break free of the bonds of slow motion, my arm may spring into action and be able to move just that bit faster, and so be able to block the oncoming ball. It seemed at the time like the only option left. As interesting as this time slowing ability seemed to be, avoiding pain took the upper hand in the decision making. So I kind of pulled my arm up harder as if I was breaking free of some string that was restraining me or someone that was holding my arm down, and broke free of the time dilation that had took me over. my arm flung up to defend my face, THWACK! The ball hit me squarely in the eye. There was no shock or wincing of pain as this moment had taken some time in arriving and was well prepared for. I knew it was the last chance, but it seems the laws of physical reality were not going to be broken that easily. The girls stormed off and I stood there for a moment soaking up what had just happened. I looked at Neil and told him of what happened, Neil said, "well, I don't know about that, but I have never seen an arm move as fast as yours just did!"

I was quite excited by this new experience and wondered what it meant, but more interestingly I found with some experimentation that I could now induce this time slowing ability at will! I needed to have a certain kind of attitude and make some physical movement to get it to kick in, but it was quite easy to achieve. I pondered the possibility of what this could do for me and decided to see if in fact it would enable me to achieve some incredible physical feats. So I tried running and breaking into slow motion, rather like the 'six million dollar man' that was on the TV in the 70's with the actor Lee Majors. But all I could tell was that I was running in slow motion, there was no way of knowing if I was actually moving any faster. So then I tried jumping, we had wooden telegraph poles between the branches on the trees which we used for playing on, and so I jumped to see if I could jump higher than the poles, but no, it seemed I could not. I got another friend Mandy to watch me as I ran, but she said all I seemed to do was have a longer stride, and didn't seem any faster.

Try as I might, I found no useful purpose for which to use this new unique but rather subjective ability. And so it slipped into the background and I stopped using it as it lost its appeal. But later on in life I saw how it could possibly have been used more usefully, if only I could still do it.

9.DOPPELGANGER

When I was in my late teens some of my sister's friends would say to me "Hey Trevor, I saw you in Guildford, I shouted hello at you, but you just ignored me, why did you ignore me?" This happened a few times, and I insisted I was not in Guildford on the days concerned. "Must be someone who looks a bit like me" I thought. But they were absolutely convinced that it *was* me and were genuinely put out as to being ignored. This was to remain a mystery for a while, maybe a month or more, I cannot remember now exactly how long, but perhaps for the summer.

Then one day I was in the second hand book store at the top of the high street, and was just about to come out, when all of a sudden walking at a fast pace was *myself* crossing the top of the high street in front of me. My doppelganger didn't see me as I was still in the shadows of the bookstore entrance, but I got a good look at *him*. I couldn't believe his eyes, it *was* me, he looked *exactly* like myself. It was so shocking I couldn't do anything accept watch as this apparition of myself strode off into the distance. He even wore a frown which was my tendency to do when rushing about. "my god, no wonder people were convinced of me ignoring them" I thought. How could it be possible? Did I have an exact twin, some dark family secret that no-one talks about? "Perhaps I'm not a product of my mother and father and actually adopted", like I did think to myself sometimes when I felt so different to everyone else. Although most of my mothers' workmates knew I was her son because of the similarity they thought, so that can't be it?

I had a feeling inside that this was the work of E.T's that somehow I had been *cloned* and it was let loose for some nefarious reason. But why clone me? And why let it loose? What was the purpose? But the fact remains, he exists, and even I was shocked at how similar he was, it was like looking into a mirror. Surely people who see others who look like them immediately *know* that it's not them by little differences? Ok he was there and gone quickly, too quickly to really check, but he didn't look friendly enough to shout at, even if I had the presence of mind to shout at him. After that year I never heard again from anyone mistaking the doppelganger for myself, he seems to have disappeared. Perhaps that's just as strange as his appearance? This was to remain a mystery to this day. A clone, a spiritual projection of myself or an evil twin? Or maybe even a friendly twin? I resigned myself to the possibility I might never know.

31

10. IQ TEST

In my late twenties I did an IQ test for MENSA the high IQ society. I always believed I was perhaps average or even a bit dim, as the rather inadequate Victorian teaching methods in the UK and useless teachers would have me believe. But on the back of 'The Sun' newspaper was a small quiz which said if you can do this, you might be eligible for entry into MENSA. I did it for a laugh and found it was easy, so thought, what the hell, I'll just send off for the home testing kit and see what my score is. Still never believing I would be eligible for actual entry into MENSA. But interested and secretly hoping I might be at least just a tad above 'average'. The test came and I did it in exactly the method as they asked and timed myself and didn't spend longer on any of the questions than I should or try to cheat. The results came back and it simply said, your IQ could be high enough to join MENSA, and was invited to sit a proper invigilated test set at London University. I couldn't hardly believe it, and so applied to go. The test went ok, but I was never any good at exams and was panicking about it, and I knew I didn't do as well as I could have done. Sure enough the test results came back and said my score was above 96% of the population but not high enough for entry into MENSA which requires a score of 98% or more. But, they said that there is a high level of underachievers in MENSA due to schools not being able to deal with fast learning students, just as they are unable to cope with slow learning students, so a lot fall out of the system and subsequently fail the first test. So they then offered a second chance, to sit another test which uses more problem solving by shapes and puzzles rather than using language and mathematics which uses education more than raw intelligence. I took this chance and sat the second test, determined to do the best I could. During this test, I began to see some of the questions and the answers almost immediately, without thinking about them. I would see a problem and see the answer immediately, but also see *ALL* the steps leading from the start to the end answer. I just did the test and felt at the end that I could not have done any better. I knew that it was the best I was capable of, whether I passed or not it didn't matter, I felt good because for once in my life I knew I did my absolute best and whatever the score was would be fine.

But the interesting thing that I found was this strange ability to see the question and steps to the answer all at once, without having to think about it and spend time trying to work it out. It wasn't on all the questions just a few that I noticed. Then I realised that some part of consciousness was working at a different level, and a different space-time to my normal everyday thinking. This was what happened that day with the tennis ball, only rather than this different space-time consciousness working in the background, my normal everyday thinking went *INTO* this mode of consciousness and stayed there until I brought myself back into the space-time consciousness of everyone else. So now the usefulness of this time slowed ability is realised, when doing tests, exams or something where quick thinking is needed, imagine if you looked at a question on the test paper, and was able to put yourself into this time slowed consciousness, you would have the ability to look at the problem for a much longer time before having to answer it.

You hear of people saying that when they had a car accident it was like it was all in slow motion, well, then it was, they obviously had managed to step into the time dilated mode of consciousness, which means it is possible probably for everyone. I have never heard of someone doing it at will before like I use to do though, and could have been a very interesting thing to analyse if I was still able to do it.

The results of the second exam came back and I found that I had an IQ which was above 98% of the rest of the population and was cordially invited to join MENSA, which I did, and stayed a member for some years. There is a subscription to pay of a nominal amount each year which was not much. I eventually didn't renew my membership because I couldn't see the point of it all. I had some grandiose idea that MENSA would be seeking to use all this incredible high powered thinking for some use, for betterment of mankind or the world, but what I found was that there was mainly lots of groups which they called sig's (special interest groups). These were groups started by members on subjects as mundane as pottery and geeky things like star trek and everything else you could imagine. These kind of groups one could join outside of MENSA, why pay a subscription every year just for a list of groups to join? Local areas had groups that met in pubs and such like, but no idea of making any use of this extraordinary high IQ, so "what's the point?" I thought to myself, and rather deflated and fed up with the organisation I decided not to continue my subscription.

11.GHOSTS, SPIRITS AND ORBS

I had quite a few experiences related to ghosts, spirits and orbs. As far as my memory serves the very first one was when I was young, not sure what age but most probably around 10yrs old. I was invited to stay at my friend's house at the end of the road where I saw or was to see, the UFO. It was a farmhouse built in the 1950's so not so old, and not somewhere you immediately associate with ghosts. My friend had a bunk bed in his bedroom and I was to have the top bunk. We stayed up and watched Dr Who on television and had Dinner and eventually retired to bed. It wasn't until we got to the bedroom and about to retire when Chris my friend said "oh, I forgot to mention, we have a ghost. Don't worry though it doesn't do any harm, it sometimes opens my bedroom door at night". Well, that's the last thing you want to hear when you are about to go bed at night, especially at such a young impressionable age. Too late to do anything about it now though, so off to bed we went. I woke up in the night, I always slept very easily, but also awoke easily at the slightest sound. I awoke to a sound of creaking. It was the creaking of the staircase, I could hear the slow creaking of each step as somebody, or something, was coming up the stairs. Then the landing floor boards creaked, gosh it's not that old a house, why do all the floorboards have to creak? My heart was beating faster as the creaks got closer, slowly the creaking came to outside the bedroom door. Sure enough just as Chris had said the bedroom door opened, I couldn't tell if the handle had turned, it must have done as the door had opened, now quite frightened and holding the bed covers tightly I whispered "chris, chris" but to no reply, he must have been fast asleep. There was no more creaking but just me wide eyed looking out from under the blankets, opposite the bunk bed in front of me was a clothes cupboard. It had one of those latches that you have to lift up so that the bar comes out of the rest, so that the door can open. I looked in astonishment as the latch lifted all on its own and the bar lifted out of the recess, and the door opened just a few inches. There was no more movement and no more creaks, it seemed to be all over, slowly my eyes became heavy and I slipped back into sleep. The next day I exclaimed to Chris what had happened and Chris replied that yes it occurs a lot, and sometimes he gets fed up with the door keep opening at night and says out loud "oh, shut the door would you!" .. and promptly evidently the door would be shut. It turns out that the family found out that one of the builders to the house committed suicide and hung himself from one of the rafters. This they felt could have been the ghost that visits Chris's room at night.

Many years later I was in Thailand, travelling around, thinking of staying and teaching English as a foreign language. I had a Thai girlfriend who lived on the outskirts of Bangkok in a house with her brother. My girlfriend, 'Nok', (not her real name so as to protect her identity), was in her early thirties and her brother was in his mid to late twenties. Unfortunately both their parents had died when they were quite young and this had left them quite traumatised. They were left the house in which they lived and it was a nice 4 bedroom house. One of the rooms however was always locked out of use. There was a shrine on the landing of the first floor and up a short staircase led to the 'locked' room. My girlfriend and her brother would be out during the day at work and I would browse the internet and meditate in front of the shrine sometimes. On one of these days I was on the internet downstairs and thought I heard movement upstairs. Perhaps in the mysterious locked room? I felt a bit un-nerved but carried on with my browsing. Then I saw a shadow move at the top of the stairs out of the corner of my eye. That was it, I had to investigate, it was after all daytime and the house was brightly lit. So I made my way upstairs and looked about. Nothing could be seen, so against my better judgement I went to the locked room and knocked on the door. No reply, so I checked the other bedrooms and there was definitely nobody home. On the return of Nok from work I had to ask about the locked room, she told me that it is where they keep all their parents stuff, they keep the room as the parents had kept it when they were alive, so that's why the door was locked and they didn't want anyone going inside to disturb it. Echo's of the movie 'Psycho' ran through my mind, but I kept pushing it out of my head. Nok assured me that no-one stayed in that room, so hearing noises, as I told her, were not possible, probably the wind or the creaking of the old wooden house. Thai people are *VERY* afraid of ghosts, and to give her the impression that the house was haunted was *not* a good idea, so I left it at that.

Nok worked as a research assistant for a big Bangkok university and as part of her job she was to go to a small town on the border of Thailand and Malaysia. There was a project there called 'rubbish for eggs'. Where the poor locals would collect rubbish and try to recycle as much as possible, and they would do this in exchange for eggs. Someone had worked out eggs had a lot of nutritional value and were very flexible in the foods that could be made from them, such as omelettes, local pancake type of foods, they also could be boiled, poached, fried etc. This proved to be quite a successful operation. So she was invited down to see the operation in action and she took me with her and we had separate rooms which were provided for us at a hotel in town. We were also invited out to visit various places on the border and had the opportunity to visit a police outpost a couple of hour's boat ride into the jungle for a short walk into the rainforest. At this outpost the only foreigners that ever went there were scientists looking for wildlife (tigers) or remote tribes which lived in the rainforest on edge of which the outpost was based. On one such trip we were invited to stay overnight at a friend's house along the border not far from an official border crossing at Hat yai. We were with a few other people and as the Thai's are actually quite conservative, the men would sleep in one room and the ladies would sleep in another separate room, hence the separate hotel rooms, as unless you were married sleeping together would be frowned upon big time.

I went to shower and clean up before bed. In Thailand you find houses that have a kind of big water container, which is not a bath, but with a bowl you scoop up the water and then proceed to pour it over yourself to wash. It's always hot especially right down in the south of Thailand so cold water is a blessing before bed to cool down. So as I started to pour water over my head I heard a 'ching' sound. At the other end of this water container, which is made of concrete and has a 4 inch thick wall, on top of the wall about waist height is the bar of soap in a metal dish. Now this container is about 6ft long and I was standing at one end of it and the soap dish was at the other end. It sounded like I or the water had knocked the dish and made the sound. But I didn't splash myself that hard and it was too far away to have been affected or for me to have knocked it. As soon as I saw the dish I knew I hadn't touched it, or that it was possible. I stopped and thought for a moment then suddenly had the feeling that I was not alone and that 'something' else had knocked the soap dish. I tried to put it out of my mind and went into the room I was to share with another man, I was alone and decided to try and rest and 'Meditate sleep'. This means to lie down meditating and to just let yourself fall into sleep. Then as I was laying there I heard something, it was a voice, but it wasn't outside of myself it was in my mind, I listened and heard a female Thai voice speaking to me. My Thai was not good enough to understand what she was saying, but I got the *'impression'* that she was asking who I was and what I was doing there. It was just a kind of *'Knowing'* of what she was saying as if we connected on some level beyond the language barrier. I came back to the very conscious level of being awake and sat up on the very thin mat on the floor which was the 'Bed' for the night. I then looked around and said out loud in my best Thai " My name is Trevor, I'm from England, here as a friend of Nok, I'm staying for one night and then going on tomorrow." I knew this was out of the way of tourists and perhaps a white foreigner had never stayed in this house before. The spirit must have been confused and intrigued as to who I was and what I was doing there. I remembered a time in my past when I lived with my Thai wife in a village in south east Thailand. There were very few foreigners that ever went there, only a German guy who had married another local girl and came to visit for holidays. I stayed in the village for some months and attracted a lot of interest because of being so white and foreign. There was a lady in the village that was quite scared of me and use to call me "The white ghost" as she believed I must be a spirit of some kind. She in all fairness was not quite all there perhaps, but the amount of interest was high even in the early 1990's. So how must have this Thai spirit have felt, coming as she most likely did from a distant past?

I had hoped that she understood what I said and settled down to sleep for the night. I slept well and awoke in the morning to a bright and warm day. If I wasn't sure about what had happened the previous night, I soon would be sure as when I was sitting down at a high chair at the breakfast bar, I suddenly felt a cold chill come over my bare leg and hand, and then a dark shadow went past me visible out of the corner of my eye. The spirit of the Thai lady was not imaginary or a visionary aspect of meditation, she was real, in the sense of a spirit being real in our reality at any rate. I guessed she must either be saying goodbye, or just letting me know of her presence. Again as the Thai's are not keen on ghosts I carefully asked Nok if she knew of the people in that house having a ghost, she said "NO WAY" in such a defiant tone that I knew, again, I should leave the subject well alone.

12.North East Thailand and the remarkable Monk

When living with Nok we decided to go for North east of Thailand on the border of Laos. Living some 12 km outside of there was a good friend of Nok called 'Nun' who is a lovely lady and put us up for a week in her house in which she lived with her parents. One of Nun's sisters was a teacher and taught at a school in the hills where kids of local ethnic minorities went. She said they have never seen in real life a foreigner or heard English spoken by a native speaker before, and so thought that it would be a good experience for the kids to have this opportunity. So I was asked if I would mind talking to the kids one day. "Of course" I said obligingly. So one morning me, Nok and Nun set off in Nuns car following Nun's sister to the school. It turns out they had set up a podium and a microphone and then gathered the whole of the school together to sit in front of me so that there could be a question and answer session. "Oh my god" I thought, I wasn't expecting this kind of reception, it's like I am a celebrity, so this is what it's like to be famous? The kids put up their hands and asked questions and I answered as best I could, trying my best to use the Queens English and not use any slang! But it wasn't as bad as I thought it would be and lasted maybe only half an hour. The principal of the school was very pleased that I had done this and given the kids a chance to see and hear English first hand, and so offered to take the group along with his deputy principal around the local areas sightseeing. We set off and visited some very nice sights and what was the largest Stupa in Thailand in Roi-Et province, inside were all gold with a spiral staircase leading to the top with some jewel at the pinnacle, all very lavish. It turns out that the principle was a Buddhist scholar and I was very interested in Buddhism, although the principal didn't speak English his deputy translated everything. The principal looked after a monk who lived alone on a hill side not far from Nun's house, he said would we like to visit him and see the site, so of course we agreed. This monk was a wandering monk and eventually came and settled on this large hill. The principal would go in the early mornings to take the monk to a town where the monk would do an alms round (walking with his bowl so that people can offer him food) and bring him back to the hill. Monks normally walk to town but this monk lives a long way from any towns. The monk taught the principal meditation and allowed him to stay overnight sometimes for all night meditation on the full moon nights. There was a small hall built on the hillside where they could hold ceremonies and pujas (a time of chanting and meditation held twice a day). He showed us around the site and there were some places with flat rocks where he said the monk and even he had maintained all night vigils meditating, and they had fantastic views. There was another place at the foot of a big tree, where he said there was an evil spirit who would come and attack you if you meditated there. The monk would not let anyone stay except himself, but the principal was proud and said that the monk let him stay there and meditate one night. But indeed he felt

40

and saw a dark shadow that came and instilled great fear, and eventually he had to leave that spot because of the fear and pressure he felt there. He said one day he would try again though, with a smile. We moved onwards snaking up the hill following a worn path, the principal pointing out spots for meditation vigils, until we reached near the top, where there were three faces carved out of stone in the hillside. They each represented something or someone of which I could no longer remember. But these were the guardians of the hill and each of the Thais did a Wai to the guardians (a Wai is putting the hands together, like in prayer in front of your heart) for respect. I felt a resistance to do this as it seemed like an out of date custom for superstitious locals, although Thai people do Wai's to each other all the time for respect. And also I felt a bit embarrassed at doing it for some reason. But now as the others were all talking in Thai together the principal explaining something, I looked at the stone faces and one of them seemed to be 'watching' me! I thought it can't be? Even though the eyes were a fixed stone carving, they *'seemed'* to be watching me. I moved to the left and right and swayed about a bit when I thought the others couldn't see me. But the eyes still followed me, everywhere I went! Now this really was *spooky*. Now I wanted to Wai to the faces as I was in fear of upsetting them as I hadn't paid my respects already, but it would look silly doing it *now*. So I waited for a moment when no-one could see me and I put my hands together and raised them to my chest and bowed slightly to the stone face that was *watching* me. Glad I had done it and no-one had seen me, so I didn't feel foolish, I looked back at the stone faces. Now it seemed that the face was *not* looking at me directly anymore. I couldn't believe it, what had happened? If the face was such that it just *seemed* that the eyes followed you like some paintings, then it would *always* seem like that? But now it wasn't *watching* me anymore. Feeling rather relieved, and a bit shocked Nun turns to me and says that they can't go any further up the hill for some reason, it's where the monk spends most of his time, I guess his private area, and *only* the monk can meditate up there, not even the principle. Not because it's private, but that for some spiritual reason and there is too strong an energy up there or something of that nature. I wasn't sure of what could be up there, but after the stone face experience I could believe it!

We set off down the hill again and the principal wanted to show us something near the bottom. We got to a rock ledge and beneath it about 15ft below was the very bottom of the hill and lots of rocks, big and small. He said in this area is where king Cobra's come to nest and bear young. Then we walked off to the right and went down to the bottom, he said not to worry they are not here now. He took us to a part of the rock face and at the bottom where his feet were, was a hole going into the rock, the first meter or so was just about large enough for a person to crawl in. He stood there with his hand leaning onto the rock face and talking, I was watching him and then also I leaned my hand onto the rock face and faced him. Nun was translating for me and evidently he was saying that in a past life he believed that he was a great King cobra snake, and he used to live here and use to go in to the rock via this hole to a larger area inside. He said that he thought there was treasure inside, hoarded by the snake that he once was. The idea of being a snake in past life intrigued me and I even thought it just *might* be possible. But when he started talking about treasure, it was becoming much more of a typical Thai style myth, why would a snake hoard treasure? Ridiculous! He went on to say that he even believed that his deputy was a snake also and that they knew each other when they were both snakes. The story was growing, and so was my incredulity! But as we were both leaning on the rock face, something happened, like the principle received some information from me through the rock, and now he looked directly at me and I could just *feel, something.* Then the principle invited us all to come and stay the night as today was the night of the full moon when they do an all night meditation vigil. Nun asked me if I was interested, and I jumped at the chance, thinking it would be fun, especially after all the ghost stories and experiences there. The principal was happy and said he just needed to ask the monk's permission for everyone to come. So we set off towards the area where the cars were parked. As we went down the path ahead I could see the monk sweeping the pathway keeping it clean, as we got nearer I could see more clearly the monks face, and I couldn't believe it. After all the principle was saying about the monk who had more than 25 years experience I was expecting an ageing man, but no, when I could see his face he looked no more than 20 years old if a day! How could that be possible? And even stranger, as I was thinking this the monk smiled. Now you could say he knew what I was thinking, or guessed, because people always thought that he looked so young! But no, I could *feel* the monk's mind inside my own, knowing my thoughts. It was no guessing, the monk could read my mind! It's as sure as day, there was no mistaking it, the monk could read thoughts! I could simply *feel* it as definite fact, this was one of strangest mind expanding experiences I have had, and I have had a lot! The monk was evidently 45 years old and I found out later that the principle had told Nun that he could read minds, that it was one of the skills that he developed naturally as the monk became more experienced in meditation. The principle also told of how he himself had developed some mind reading skills, but not to the level of the monk. The monk had been teaching the principle for some years now and would entrust him to lead the night's meditation in the absence of the monk who was going to stay at the very top of the hill and meditate alone up there for the night.

I felt excited about coming back that night and wondered if I would get the spot on the hillside that overlooked the jungle and impressive views, you evidently could see the sun rise in the morning from there. Wow, what an opportunity! They all went their separate ways agreeing to come back again meeting at about

7.30pm that evening. Myself, Nok, Nun and her family were all having dinner that evening and discussing the day's events when Nun told me that the principle had said he knew that I had *seen* the snakes myself. That's odd I thought, it must have been when we were both leaning on the rock face, because I noticed the principle looking at me, and felt that he was *seeing* something, but didn't know what. But I didn't know what he meant by me having seen the snakes, so I shrugged my shoulders and said "I don't know what he means?" we carried on with dinner, and then all of a sudden I remembered something that happened about 10 years previously.

Let me explain ....

I had started meditation as I believed that it was the key to the door, to the place where all my unanswered questions could be answered. After travelling down the science route where it gets interesting at the quantum level, I realised that although it got interesting it didn't have *answers*. I then went down the route of philosophy and esoteric philosophy where interesting things could be found and I even had some startling experiences whilst following P.D Ouspensky's directions.

13. Three Experiences through esoteric practice

Three startling and interesting experiences were achieved by following the advice of Ouspensky through his books. It is hard for me to remember all the details of what practice I had to go through to achieve the results, but anyone can read Ouspensky's books and find the practices, probably written in 'the Fourth way'. But here's the first of the three I experienced. It was to see yourself, your true self. Not the self that you think is you, but the one hidden from your everyday view of yourself. Most of what I could remember about the practices was that one had to watch one's self, all the time. So you would go about your daily business as normal, but pay special attention to what you were feeling. If you were walking along a path outside for example, you would say to yourself "walking, this is how it feels when I'm walking". Then you must notice yourself walking, and also the feeling of movement. You would notice all the senses, by saying to yourself, "I am Hearing" as you notice the sound of cars passing by. You would say to yourself "seeing, I am seeing" and mentally note the experience of seeing the sights and colours and shapes of the world around you. "feeling" feeling the cold wind biting the cheeks of your face, the ground beneath your feet etc. "breathing" that you are breathing and noticing the in and out of your breath. "Thinking", the thoughts that pass through your mind, the simple act of doing this practise. And so it would go on, this was actually quite difficult to do when you were working, and I found myself being distracted from my actual work as I tried to follow this practice, but determination was something I could most definitely muster when I wanted to. And so I carried on. Then one day as I was practising, something happened, I suddenly saw a *monster!* Yes, it was the most horrible thing I had ever seen in my life, it was horrible, evil, so much so, that in fact if I were to look at it for more than the

45

briefest of moments to which I was allowed to see it, I would most assuredly have gone *mad*. That was the power of this monster, and the horror which was attached to it. There was a reason that it was *so* horrible, a reason that I couldn't look at it for more than a second. The reason was even more shocking, because the monster was *Me*. Yes, it was myself, what I saw was all the nasty and hurtful things that I had said, and all the hurtful and nasty things I had ever done in my whole life. They were all kept together in some dark place, of the mind, or of the collective unconscious, it couldn't be known. The fact remained that everything you say and do is recorded, somewhere, and can be retrieved and looked at, at any time. This was all the bad things, not the good, whether it was just filtered so that I could only experience the bad things, or it was a separate place from where the good things are stored I couldn't know. This was a revelation, shocking and life altering. Surely after this one could not be the same anymore, you would watch everything you said and did, knowing that it is all remembered, logged and not forgotten. It made me vow to be a better person. To watch what I said, and how I acted towards people, never would life be the same again. If only everyone were allowed to experience this, about their own lives, we would not treat each other in the same way. We would all be much more respectful and forgiving. Perhaps even wars could be a thing of the past? Or is that too far? No, you would see all the death and destruction, all the faces you have killed even by proxy, surely it would be an end to all wars! I felt after a while that this was a surely a gift to me, after being scolded by the impressions and reality of the facts of what I had done, I knew it was a chance to change, to be a better person. I certainly was now, changed forever. Well, you would think that, but what I found was that after a while the pain recedes, and then one continues to act in the old pattern of thinking and actions. But then one remembers, and has a new burst of good actions and speech. But this is how it goes on, until one change's more permanently. But still I needed to remind myself

46

occasionally. This is how things are for all people, we forget so easily, some tragedy in the news and we vow to be more careful ourselves, but then a few weeks go by and the victims are all forgotten and we fall back into our old ways. Why are we so forgetful? It seems that we are bombarded with so many sensory impingements that it's impossible to remember everything, even things we thought so important last week, last month. But surely this would last forever, no, not so, over the years I would forget until something caused me to remember.

The second Experience was still following the basic same methods, but you held in your mind a certain outcome to which you wanted to achieve. There was written that you could vastly improve your eyesight, so that you could see very far into the distance, like using a telescope or high powered binoculars. That the limits of our physical bodies were more of a psychological limit rather than a physical one. I would take my dog 'Shandy' for regular walks about the village and try to practice as he went. Then one day I was on one of my regular walks and all of a sudden my vision shot forwards down the path some 300 meters or so and I saw very clearly like my eyes had a telescopic function, to the motorcycle shop ahead. It lasted only a couple of seconds and my vision retracted back to my 'normal' vision. This was a revelation, I was excited it actually worked, but I did have belief, as this was highly important, without it, it may not have been possible. I also remembered reading that to over use this function may cause some permanent damage to the eyes, which would mean that perhaps it's not meant to be used much, if at all. But the fact is, it *is* possible. I didn't try to do this again as it takes a long time to get to fruition and was not a useful tool, but merely was an experiment in what is possible.

The third experience again was the same watching of one's self over time during all aspects of everyday life, but it was to see the world rather differently, to see what is filtered out. The mind filters out everything that you don't need to know for basic survival. But the eyes and the mind 'sees' so much more than what we consciously perceive. The idea is to break down the filters and 'see' more of everything that is actually taken in before it gets 'filtered' by the mind. So while practising this during work one day I went to the cafeteria for a break with my work friends. To my surprise when I looked at my work colleague that I was particularly friendly with, she 'looked' different. It was very hard to explain, but she kind of 'glowed' with a bright luminosity. Her face was the same, but looked different, it looked much better, kind of perfect. It was as if I could see the 'real' inner self of someone. They looked like themselves but also they didn't. It was the most strange and wonderful experience. It lasted again quite briefly, perhaps only 30 seconds or a minute, but it was a beautiful experience. It could have been that *everything* looked somehow different. But the effect did not last long enough to really look around, I was so astounded just looking at my friend. So these were the three experiences gained by following the esoteric philosophies.

14.Religion

But It still didn't really deliver the answers I was looking for, but because Ouspensky's teacher Gurdjeff had gleaned most, if not all he knew from religious and mystic men, it lead me onto looking at religion. Whilst investigating religion I looked at Hinduism and bought a book called 'The Upanishads' translated by Eknath Easwaran, India's loftiest philosophy, more than 3000 years old, they are the earliest living records of what Aldous Huxley called 'The perennial philosophy'. In this book I read things like this:

*"An immediate practical consequence for human happiness is that the reason we try to get pleasure from outside satisfactions is we are victims of an enormous fallacy: we believe there **is** an "outside" apart from us. But we carry the world within us, and thus the source of all human fulfilment, all Love, all creativity."*

(From The" Upanishads" on The Aitareya Upanishad-by Eknath Easwaran pg 123)

Reading this book was the first time I really felt like something *opened* in my mind, I felt that I really understood what was being said by those scribes thousands of years ago. They talked of a place called the *"real"* and that this life and plane of existence is the *"unreal"*. I really felt I knew the place described as the real, it was *Home,* yes, not here but there in those words I recognised and felt the real *home.* So now I knew where I was trying to get to. All this searching was to get to somewhere and now I had found it, I didn't know it, but in fact all this time I was trying to get home. The place described by those mystics was it, there was no doubt. My mind now opened and focused on where I wanted to get to. But the one thing was missing, how to get *there?* Ok so they used meditation that was the way. But what was completely lacking was a practical method of meditation, how *exactly* to do it? This led me on a voyage of discovery that was to take in places in the Far East, in which time I discovered Buddhism in Thailand, which has a very clear method of meditation and a philosophy which agreed with my own, of peace, not killing or harming anyone or any animal, of love and respect of all things. So meditation was the key to getting home, and to all the answers that I needed. I got back to the UK and was meditating, I used to drive to a car park in a wood in my lunchtimes from work, eat my sandwich and then settle down to meditating sitting in the driver's seat of my car. This was quite successful and I could feel even though it was only 20-30 minutes a day it was making a difference. I definitely seemed to have a knack for meditating, if indeed there is such a knack? One day I finished my meditating and was driving back to work and I felt this wave wash over me. It was like someone pouring over me a bucket of calm, yes, of calm, I just suddenly felt all my body relax and my mind felt calm. I didn't realise that my body was tense, but it must have been because now it was relaxed and I could feel the difference. I guess if you live all your life tensed up, you don't know what relaxed is? It was amazing, I knew it was the result of all this time meditating, and just gave me the spur to carry on and try harder. So now with renewed confidence I carried on meditating, using any spare half hour to sit down and meditate. I thought I might get that calm feeling again, but it never came back. I would eventually learn that experiences are never repeated, and to expect a repeat is a sure fire way to get nothing at all. One has to have the completely open mind of expecting and wanting *nothing*. So, one lunchtime I was sitting again in my car meditating, letting go of everything, when a vision popped into my mind's eye. The whole of my inner vision was taken up with an eye, that's right, an eye. It was huge, massive. The only way to describe it is like if you were standing on the edge of very high mountain, and all that you could see was sky in front of you. Now replace that sky with the image of an eye, and then you would have an approximation of what I saw. But this eye was no ordinary eye, it was not human! It was green in colour and the pupil was not round, but elliptical from top to bottom, like a reptile. There was a feeling that came with this vision. But there was not any emotion, like no emotion at all. Patience is what was coming through, something, someone, was watching, very patiently watching with no emotion. As I realised what was there I tried to grasp the image with my mind. A difficult thing to explain, but to meditate successfully you have to let go of everything, feelings, thoughts, emotions, pictures, *everything*. So when this simply popped up in front of me, it was just there, I didn't try to analyse it or study it, because I was in a state of letting go. But this was all of a sudden *there*, so I naturally just went to *look* at it. At that point I was trying to grasp it with my mind to analyse it, and no sooner had the *intention* been to do that, it was gone. My meditation was of course finished at that point. I opened my eyes and sat there for a moment, stunned. I started to drive back to work, but then, I tried to analyse what I saw. The more I thought about it, the more it scared me. I wasn't asleep, I was *very* awake, and yet what did it mean? Flooding into my mind came UFO's and their illusive occupants, the watchers as I thought of them. That was what this eye was doing, *watching,* was it then an alien? Could it belong to what in UFO lore is known as the reptilian race, a race of bipedal reptilians that could be according to some perhaps the original species and occupants of planet earth? It could be that what I saw was a representation of the fact that I am under constant observation. Maybe then it's a warning, they are trying to stop me from meditating, and therefore possibly escaping this illusory realm, by breaking free from the mental bonds that bind us? Or is it that I had somehow seen the bug/tracker that is attached to me and keeping tabs on my whereabouts, and this was represented by one of their eyes? Or was it a memory, one of being abducted, tested on and probed by them? Or is it that my real inner self is not human but alien, my inner mind or being that is watching, meditating, or perhaps there is a part of all humans that is reptilian? It could of course be benevolent and simply watching out of interest or a willingness to help, or perhaps knows that I am in some way important? So many questions but not enough answers. Too many negative possibilities, in fact, so many that it scared me into not meditating for a couple of years. I realised that I needed guidance, someone to guide me through the maze of things that can happen, and to tell me what it was I was experiencing, seeing! It seems I was *too* good at meditating, and got ahead of myself and into trouble already. I had read in some places that meditating can be dangerous and a guide should be sought. You don't often read that, but they were right, I needed a Guide.

My artistic impression of the eye I saw in meditation, the meditating monk representing myself in meditation.

I was still eating dinner at Nun's house, and then suddenly I remembered that time back in the car park, the vision of the eye. Of course! That must be it. The principle must have somehow seen that vision I had, or got a feeling of it anyway. If he did, then perhaps he thought that I was a snake too in the past, or that I had some vestigial memory of it? Either way, to know of a meditational experience of someone, especially from years ago shows that he must have a great ability, one presumably brought on by an ability to have very deep meditation, it was impressive. Even if it was nothing to do with snakes, still impressive! I went to speak out and said "Oh, yes I remember something". Everyone looked up, and Nun said to me "No, you shouldn't speak of any experience in meditation, you should just keep it to yourself". So I said "oh, ok" and did just that. That evening they went in the car to go back to the hill for the night's meditation. Now I was actually rather nervous, I thought "oh, what if he actually does give me that ledge overlooking the jungle valley to meditate on?" It was a good 5 minutes for anyone to reach me if I shouted out. If a snake had bitten me or any number of nightly forest visitors that might stumble across me sitting there. It was becoming more of a scary thought that anything else now, very dark and spooky, especially with those pesky ghosts or bad spirits. I found all my bravado had disappeared, I was now hoping that I *wouldn't* be left alone *anywhere*, everything seems much different in the inky blackness of night!

When we arrived at the hill, we met other people who had come to join in the night's activities. We all set off towards the sala hall, which had a large Buddha inside. Nok told me that we would be spending the night in the Sala, and doing sitting and walking meditation just outside the Sala. But after that at about midnight we would all settle inside the sala for sleeping meditation. Which basically means we won't be awake all night but falling asleep mindfully. Phew, what a relief! I thought. Now I could laugh at myself about actually being worried about what I thought was a good idea earlier in the day. It was a good night and I enjoyed it immensely but it was to pass without any incident. The only excitement came from wanting the toilet in the middle of the night, everyone was asleep and the toilet was a small wooden shack 20 meters from the sala. It meant having to go outside and brave the dark forest night, with the wind batting the trees and sounds all around, again I found myself scared of going, but I had to, no way could I hold it till the morning, flipping small bladder! So out I went, trying to hurry, and running back laughing to myself of how ridiculous I am at being so scared.

Eventually I heard from Nun, that the Principal had continued to dig out the entrance under the rock and had indeed found jewellery in there. He gave some of the jewellery away to friends and people he thought were snakes with him in his previous life including the vice principal. I still didn't know what to make of this incredible story. The principle seemed like an honest and caring person, why would he lie? But I had my natural scepticism rise in my mind, although my experience was *other* than normal with those people at that place. I decided with this new news to leave it as an open end to this incredible adventure and not to decide either way the veracity of this information until or unless more evidence comes to light in the future.

15.Monastic life

Continuing with the theme of Ghosts and spirits, I was to become a novice Buddhist monk in the Thai tradition of forest monks, which is a contemplative tradition. While I was there I had an encounter with a spirit. I used to go for a short 40 minute nap after lunch, and it was on one of these days that I had a most unusual experience. I had settled down on the small mattress on the floor of my room and was letting myself go. I was not asleep yet, but in the in-between state in which many experiences can come when the still conscious mind is touching on the subconscious. As I lay there on my left side a strange feeling started to come over me. I noticed that my face kind of scrunched up a bit and my back started to arch, like I was an old man, and then I heard a voice which said "hello me old mate", but this voice, I could hear it, but not in my head, I could actually *hear* it. Then I realised that the voice came out of my own mouth. More than that but whomever this spirit may be, was taking over my body and speaking to me using my own vocal chords. This just felt creepy, too much for me and when I realised what was happening I kind of tensed up and managed to push the spirit out of my body. After a minute to compose myself and let the experience of what just happened sink in. I thought "no. I can't have that, it's too much". So I said out loud "don't do that again, I don't mind if you are friendly, but don't try to take over my body, I don't like it". Whoever the spirit was certainly seemed friendly and said hello in a way as if he *knew* me. But I did not recognise the voice or feel any recognition of who this spirit might have *been*. The spirit never took over, or even tried to take over my body again. He may have been around, but that was the last direct contact I felt from this being. But those 40 minute naps turned out to be very eventful times.

Again when I was lying down after lunch in a very relaxed way I experienced something new. My mind was clear and everything was dark, as I lay with my eyes closed. Then all of a sudden I was travelling down a dark tunnel, in my mind. This seemed like a narrow dark tunnel and I was shooting down it at quite a pace. Then I came out of the other end, into a large dark area, all was blackness, except for in front of me was a shape, not symmetrical but like a hole in broken glass in a kind of fallen over figure of eight shape or perhaps like the infinity shape. Around the edges of this shape were what looked like cracks, splitting out into the darkness. But *inside* the shape was another place entirely, it was like looking through a window to somewhere else. There was a scene, like looking at a television. In the scene was a plain of grass. And bent down on their haunches were a load of kids, dressed in scout's uniforms. They were all searching the grass for something it seemed, but for what I had no idea. And I could see the back of an adult, standing over the kids watching them, perhaps directing them? I got the feeling this person was female, although I only saw her back, in a light brown shirt and the back of her neckerchief could be seen. Well, this was a cheap TV because there was no sound! But it was at least in colour! This was very intriguing, and I was fully conscious of myself and the scene. It was like one of my life dreams, with a certain *real* quality about it. Then I thought ok this is interesting, let's see if I can go through that window like area and investigate the scene from the inside. But as soon as I tried to push my consciousness through the window I was expelled from the vision and back to my room.

It turns out this was not a one off event, as on another day I found myself shooting down that same tunnel and out into the large inky black void. This time there was no window, but instead was an amazing sight. Hanging in the inky blackness was no less than Stonehenge! But the massive stones were not just floating around in space on their own, they were all still firmly on the green grass of ground we know them to be on. But the ground only extended just outside of the stones, then the ground underneath was dark earth that tapered down to a point directly underneath the middle of the circle approximately slightly deeper than the stones were tall on the surface. But there was one very obvious difference to the stones, on one of them was what looked like etched into the face of the stone was a spiral!? All of this vision was simply hanging there in this massive black space. It was like I was standing at the edge of a massive cavern containing all this as when I looked down I could see those cracks again. Like the darkness had been hit and had the splintered cracks like seen on a glass window that has been hit hard and hasn't broken, but cracked all over. These cracks went off into the distance towards the hanging Stonehenge, but disappearing from view before getting that far. What could this mean? There must be a purpose, a reason for seeing this? I decided to try and walk on the cracked blackness with my mind, but as I did I again was expelled from the area and back into my room.

Although these two events seemed like they must be important, or showing me something of value, I couldn't work it out, and still to this day I am waiting for the answers and reasons to come to light about those visions. I did discover that American shaman Indians use to have the same experience of shooting down the narrow tunnel and seeing the future through a window, or getting some answer to some question. I had definitely never heard of or read of this before, and found that particularly interesting that I should have a shared experience with shamans of another country. This puts their experience into an interesting new light as they were obviously telling the truth. But why should I experience that? Was I a shaman in a past life? Or a common experience to mystics, shamans and spiritual practitioners the world over? Still more questions that need to be answered.

One point of interest came when learning the chanting and replies to questions when one becomes ordained into the Sangha of Monks. There is a ritual which one needs to go through to be formerly accepted into the Sangha and in this ritual is some poignant questions such as 'do you have leprosy?' But there is one question which stood out as rather odd, it is 'are you a human?' below is the list of questions that are asked:

Instructing the applicant outside the gathering: (Mv.I.76.7)

Suṇasi (Naga) ayan-te sacca-kālo bhūta-kālo. Yaṃ jātaṃ taṃ saṅgha-majjhe pucchante. Santaṃ atthīti vattabbaṃ. Asantaṃ n'atthīti vattabbaṃ. Mā kho vitthāsi. Mā kho maṅku ahosi. Evan-taṃ pucchissanti: Santi te evarūpā ābādhā?

Listen, Naga. This is your time to tell the truth, to tell what is factual. Things that have occurred will be asked about in the Community. [Or, You will be asked in the Community about things that have occurred.] Whatever is right should be affirmed. Whatever is not right should be denied. Do not be embarrassed. Or ashamed. They will ask you as follows: Do you have any diseases such as these?

Question:	*Answer:*
Kuṭṭhaṃ?	N'atthi, bhante.
Gaṇḍo?	N'atthi, bhante.
Kilāso?	N'atthi, bhante.
Soso?	N'atthi, bhante.
Apamāro?	N'atthi, bhante.
Manusso'si?	Āma, bhante.
Puriso'si?	Āma, bhante.
Bhujisso'si?	Āma, bhante.
Anaṇo'si?	Āma, bhante.
N'asi rāja-bhaṭo?	Āma, bhante.
Anuññāto'si mātā-pitūhi?	Āma, bhante.
Paripuṇṇa-vīsati vasso'si?	Āma, bhante.
Paripuṇṇan-te patta-cīvaraṃ?	Āma, bhante.

Kin-nāmo'si?	Ahaṃ bhante (Naga) nāma.
Ko nāma te upajjhāyo?	Upajjhāyo me bhante āyasmā (*Varapanno*) nāma.
Leprosy?	*No, sir.*
Boils?	*No, sir.*
Eczema?	*No, sir.*
Tuberculosis?	*No, sir.*
Epilepsy?	*No, sir.*
Are you a human being?	*Yes, sir.*
Are you a man?	*Yes, sir.*
Are you a free man?	*Yes, sir.*
Are you free from debt?	*Yes, sir.*
Are you exempt from government service?	*Yes, sir.*
Do you have your parents' permission?	*Yes, sir.*

Are you fully 20 years old?	*Yes, sir.*
Are your bowl and robes complete?	*Yes, sir.*
What is your name?	*Venerable sir, I am named (*Naga*).*
What is your preceptor's name?	*Venerable sir, my preceptor is named (Varapanno).*

Everything that is done or said or asked has a history and story attached to it and the question 'are you a human?' is no different, the story goes like this:

... Once a Naga, a powerful serpent who can take the form of a human being, was mistakenly ordained as a monk. Shortly after, when asleep in his hut, the Naga returned to the shape of a huge snake. The monk who shared the hut was somewhat alarmed when he woke up to see a great snake sleeping next to him! The Lord Buddha summoned the Naga and told him he may not remain as a monk, at which the utterly disconsolate snake began to weep. The snake was given the Five Precepts as the means to attaining a human existence in his next life when he can then be a monk. Then out of compassion for the sad snake, the Lord Buddha said that from then on all candidates for the monkhood be called 'Naga' as a consolation. They are still called 'Naga' to this day.

Adherents to the idea of shape-shifting reptilian beings may be interested in this, and it may point to a historical event as the Buddha was practical in every sense and didn't say something merely for effect. So the idea of reptilians and their ability to disguise themselves as humans by powerful psychic means seems like it may have some historical premise, if this story is taken at face value.

I had found a good friend and comrade in another novice monk who came to the monastery, His name is Eduardo and he is from Portugal. I found out that he had also seen UFO's, well, more felt them, as when he was coming to the Monastery he went on a trip through Europe and when in the south of France he felt the wind of what seemed like low flying birds going over his head. He looked but saw nothing, then took a photo of the beautiful valley in front of him. But on looking back at the photo's he had caught two UFO's that had obviously just flown over his head and were heading down the valley (These photo's are his private ones and he is keeping them for his own book, so unfortunately I cannot share them here). Large disc shaped objects, that were completely invisible to the eye, but this opened up his mind to the reality of the phenomena. Together, myself and Eduardo set about taking photos of the skies around the monastery, seeing things in the shapes of flying birds and insects, and sometimes something more interesting but inconclusive. But we discovered that we seemed to get a lot of what are known as 'Orbs'. Especially in the temple or when a lot of people were coming. Note that not that the people were there yet, but the night before would always see an increase in Orb activity. Some people say all orbs are just the reflection of light from the flash of the camera bouncing off of floating dust particles in the air. And there is no doubt that that does indeed give pictures of orb like anomalies, but not *all* are simply dust particles. Some behave in ways contrary to floating dust, by speeding around in a very fast motion leaving orbs with streaks of light trailing behind, while others are stationary, also different colours and patterns can be found. But more than this I know of the real existence of orbs because I have *seen* them with my naked eye, without flashing lights and cameras. The first experience I remember was at my friend's house in Swindon, Wiltshire. I was staying there for a few days before going to the monastery to ordain. As I sat in my bedroom I saw suddenly a light come through the wall in front of me. It was a bright round light and as soon as I saw it, it suddenly rushed straight at me. The light went straight towards my head and before I could think or do anything it went straight through my head! I knew that it had because as it passed through my head I saw the light as if it lit up the whole of the inside of my mind, before passing through and out the back of my head.

Another definitive time I saw orbs with my own eyes was on a trip to Spain, to attend a meditation retreat, headed by my old Monastic mentor. I was due to fly out from Luton airport with my friends to Spain, when at the airport I realised that I had left my passport behind. This was quite a drawback as arrangements had been made for transporting everyone from the airport to the retreat centre where the meditation retreat was to take place. I was able however to get a later flight arriving at Madrid airport late at night. There was not unfortunately any way to get me from the airport to the town of Escorial where the retreat was taking place except by train or bus. The last bus and train had left for Escorial that day, so I had to spend the night in the airport and wait for the first train in the morning. I had a night of little sleep, but felt ok in the morning when it was time for the first train. It was still dark when I arrived in Escorial, I had some vague directions to where the retreat centre was, but didn't want to get there too early, so I wandered the town looking at the sights and watching the sun rise. I found a place to have breakfast and drink some coffee to wake myself, and after feeling refreshed decided to try to find the retreat centre. It was while I was wandering around the town that I saw the orbs. At one point I stood and was wondering whether to go straight on or turn right down some steps onto a main road and follow it, whilst looking for the road the centre was on. Then off to my right hand side I saw a gathering of orbs, about 3 or 4 of them together in a bunch, they were high up a wall to the right of the steps and only moving slightly but maintaining a steady position. I could see them from the corner of my eye, I turned to look at them which I could for a brief few moments and then they disappeared. I thought that this seemed like a sign, and felt that they were trying to help me find the right direction, so I decided to take the steps to the right and along the main road. This was indeed the right direction and I soon found the correct road on which had the retreat centre. I was to see orbs and movements of things around me, some that couldn't quite be made out, for the rest of my life, but these were a couple of times when there was no mistaking the orbs. They were certainly not reflection of light off of dust particles, they were largish, about the size of a softball and not imaginary. I certainly seemed to see more odd things when I was tired, It's not my imagination, but I believe that when I'm tired and the mind wants to sleep it lets go of some of the filters that normally stop a person from seeing these things as seeing these things are not necessary for survival. It's all subjective of course, but this is what I think.

My drawing of my vision when I passed through the tunnel into the void.

My vision of Stonehenge hanging in the void with the spiral carved on one of the stones. I couldn't say that was the exact stone I saw the spiral on, I think the importance is just simply the connection between Stonehenge and the spiral.

Blue Orb taken by me at the Monastery

Red Orb taken by Dhammiko I'm on the left, taken at the Monastery

Another Red Orb this time taken by me at the Monastery

Green Orb taken by me at the Monastery with Eduardo (Dhammiko) in the background.

White Orb taken by myself at the Monastery

White Orbs taken by myself at the Monastery with Eduardo in the background

I took this in Escorial, Spain on the way to the retreat.

Here is an interesting picture taken by Eduardo in Portugal 2005, I am the one wearing the cap and sunglasses. This orb was taken and no flash was used, as you can see the robe is still in shadow. This is not then an artefact of dust reflecting the light of a flash.

16. Another Close Encounter

Whilst I was a novice at the monastery, I got to take my Mentor and Teacher to a house that was left to the monastery by a benefactor for a private 10 day retreat. My mentor was to have a silent retreat and I would make him breakfast and lunch and attend to his needs. I would knock on the door to give him his food and he would take it, all without speaking. This house was only about 1 mile from Rendlesham forest, where the UK's 'Roswell' took place. A UFO was seen on 2 nights in 1980 in the forest outside of Woodbridge Air force base which was occupied by the 67th Aerospace Rescue and Recovery Squadron, which answered only to the Department of Defence in Washington D.C. also unknown to the people of the UK at the time, was the fact it was holding nuclear weapons, and quite possibly the reason for the interest shown by the UFO. This is one of the best recorded cases in the UK and even the world due to the number of reliable and trained observers of military personnel that witnessed and chased the UFO through the forest. An audio tape was also recorded by Colonel Charles Halt as he led the team through the forest which is undeniable proof of the incident, alongside the paper trail left as they reported the incident to Washington and the UK MOD. This area of Norfolk is a 'hotspot' for UFO activity and in fact all sorts of paranormal activity. As legends of 'shuck' a large black dog which rampaged through the local towns is a historical record, and other strange creatures seen in Rendlesham forest. The house was on its own, not far from the sea, in fact when we arrived at the house we sat up drinking tea and looking out at the sea from the upstairs studio window. The benefactor was an artist and had a studio upstairs. It also had a bedroom upstairs next to the studio where Ajahn Nyanarato (my mentor) was to stay. I had a bedroom on the ground floor. That first night we stayed up till midnight, chatting and drinking tea, Ajahn was to start his 10 day silent retreat the next day and after midnight we went to bed. I was meditate sleeping and was not yet asleep when I saw through my closed eyelids a light flashing around. As I was in a semi-conscious state I ignored it. But then there was flashing again that I could see through my closed eyes. So now I was in a much more aroused state. Then by the time the lights were seen for a third time through my eyelids I was totally awake and conscious. This time I wondered what was going on and opened my eyes. To my surprise the room was full of light. This light was not a normal torch or headlight kind of light, but extremely bright, brighter than daylight, and a very white light. It completely filled the room, My bed lie along the back wall, and at the foot of my bed was the doorway. On the opposite wall to the bed was a window. Through this window is where the light appeared to be coming in, as I could see that the curtains were lit up behind. There was no sound and I could hear no one moving about. Then all of a sudden, it was as though I blinked, and the light was gone. I was sitting up in bed and now a bit afraid to move. I studied the doorway to my room waiting to see some movement or hear something, but there was nothing. I felt rather afraid, and eventually lay back down and went to sleep. Outside the window to my room about 5 feet from the window were large fir trees, I checked out the area and found no footprints or car tracks. It couldn't have been a car because there were the trees in the way. The light could only have come into the window like that from directly above the house. If it was a helicopter I would have heard it, there were helicopters that flew in from the sea and towards the old military base, and you could hear them from miles away, so I would have heard a helicopter if it was hovering over the roof of the house. Whatever it was, was totally silent.

There was another thing now as well, I could feel a presence in the house, just in the downstairs of the house. It was a strong presence, so strong that I felt that I could point to the exact area where this invisible being was. Not only that, but I felt that it was *short!* About 3 to 4 feet tall, it was all rather bizarre. I felt that the white light was connected to a UFO, but at the time I only thought that the presence I felt in the house was of a ghost or spirit. I didn't realise the effect on me until the night time, as I found that I was afraid to go to sleep, and was afraid of the dark! So much so, that I had to leave a light on at night for the remainder of time I was to stay at the house. "But I'm a grown man", I thought to himself, it's ridiculous, never the less, I had to have the light on and felt afraid. Something had definitely happened that night. At one point I decided to sleep upstairs on the sofa that was in the studio outside of Ajahn's room, because of the feeling of the presence downstairs and the fear of the night I felt. I couldn't talk to Ajahn, because he was on his retreat, and what would I say? It would sound ridiculous! I would have to wait until he finished his retreat and ask him if he saw anything that first night. So I felt better upstairs, safer, and tried to settle down on the sofa. But I couldn't, I just felt uncomfortable, *something* was stopping me from being able to sleep? It became so bad and I felt so tired that I knew I would have to go back downstairs to the bedroom down there. I also felt that this was what the being downstairs *wanted*. That somehow it couldn't watch me if I slept upstairs and wanted me to sleep downstairs. Although I really didn't want to, I eventually gingerly went back downstairs to sleep in the bedroom on the ground floor, the feeling was stronger than I could resist. This is how it was for the next few nights, and during the day I could feel a presence at certain times. Once Ajahn had finished his retreat I asked him if he remembered seeing any strange lights on that first night, or any sounds. But unfortunately he said he didn't hear or see anything. I explained what happened and about the feeling of a presence that I felt downstairs. Ajahn said he would meditate downstairs and see if he could *feel* anything there, but although he said he may have seen a light, apart from that he said he felt nothing. But actually the feeling of a presence was gone for a few days before. On the last day before we left the house Ajahn said we would do a chanting for the spirit if there is one there, I agreed and felt better for doing it. So we chanted a few parittas (prayers) before leaving. I was to investigate my feelings of the incident with the white light, and found that I *felt* like it was someone who for some reason had detected my presence there and came down to investigate. Then upon realising it was me, felt satisfied in a way of 'oh, it's ok it's only Trevor' and then left. It seems strange but this was the feeling I was left with. Not a scary feeling or one of having been abducted, which is what the evidence points to on first observation. But abduction cannot be ruled out as it's unknown if there was any missing time and false memories are normally implanted or blocked of the event.

The presence which I thought was a ghost or spirit on reflection looks also typical of an abduction scenario, as sometimes people who have been abducted have said that one of the aliens is sent to 'observe' the abductee for several days after the event. The purpose is unknown, but believed to be as a protocol to make sure the subject has not been harmed by the procedure and has settled back into it's environment comfortably. Even perhaps to make sure the incident is not reported and made a subject of investigation, which it wasn't of course because of the situation. And the presence was only there for a few days, also the presence was giving the strong impression of a being of small stature, which again lends support to the alien theory as many reports of short aliens abound, especially in the abduction field.

Ordinance survey map with the pin showing where I stayed the night I had the bright light experience at night near where the famous Rendlesham Forest UFO case took place.

17.Angels and Devas

What are Orbs? This is a question that has plagued my mind for some time. I have seen them with my own eyes, so they have a reality in what's called the *real* world. Of course everything we see is actually the minds interpretation of electrical impulses received via the optic nerve from the eye, and then everything that is received is not permitted to be acknowledged by the conscious mind and is thus *filtered* by the mind as to what we *need* to see for our basic survival. So in fact *everything* we see is subjective and also not the whole story, this is a scientific medical fact. But let's stick with observed phenomena as being part of what we call the real world for arguments sake.

Myself and Eduardo had gone about the monastery clicking away with our digital cameras and caught many an orb either in fast movement or hovering in various places. We also observed orbs of different colours, we caught red, blue, green, yellow and the obligatory white. Some also had more interesting patterning in them, and some even had what looked for all the world like faces made of two dots and a line for a mouth. Were they spirits of some previously incarnated person who has now left the mortal body and is floating around in a different form? Some perhaps, we guessed. But what is also a possibility is that some are beings naturally in a different form, a form of pure energy that is hard for us to see in our low vibrational state. As I looked through the Pali cannon I found stories of what the Buddhist scholars call Deva's. They are beings of a different form to us humans, and live in a different realm, but can connect and converse with us if they so wished. One of the interesting things about these beings is that it is told that they can be of different colours. And the colours are represented in the different colours that we captured with our cameras. Could they be the Devas as told about? One time I was lying in my bed trying to sleep but just couldn't sleep, I could not pinpoint what was stopping me from sleeping. Then all of a sudden *it* stopped, the '*it*' was vibration. The whole of my body was vibrating, every inch of me was vibrating, the only reason I knew it was vibrating was because it all of sudden *stopped* vibrating. What was the cause of the vibration? Could it be that because of my spiritual endeavours I literally was raising my vibrational level? Or was *something* raising my spiritual vibrational level? Could it be the Devas's's? Something else happened that made me wonder. One day I was waking from sleep and I could hear a voice, not like the voice of the spirit that tried to enter me as before. This time it was in my mind, but not my imagination, I could tell, the experience is totally different. This voice was singing, it was a simple song, something of what I could remember before it faded was something like "you have to be strong, to be good, you have to be good, to be strong ..." but then my memory and the voice faded out. So this voice, this being, was singing to me in my sleep. The voice was like nothing I had ever heard in my life. It was the *sweetest* voice ever. The only thing that came close to the sound that I could compare was that of a top choir boy singing, when they sound very sweet and beautiful. But even that was not *as* sweet or beautiful as the voice that I heard. It was so beautiful it made a tear come to my eye. It was singing a song of encouragement, a song to help me to carry on with my chosen spiritual path. But who was that being singing? I thought that it sounded like what in my imagination an Angel or perhaps a Deva would sound like, perhaps female? But this was all supposition as I didn't know, and never would find out who the kind, sweet encouraging voice belonged to. But who knows, life is not over yet and as sure as eggs are eggs more experiences are still to follow, and maybe the identity of that sweet sounding being will be found out eventually.

18.Meditation

Meditational experiences are completely subjective, even though there are steps that are laid out in the Pali cannon of stages or points which can be reached on the way to enlightenment, every person's experience of that stage or level is completely individual to that person. This is because of the individual nature of our psychology and personalities and likes and dislikes and the filters that we have in our minds. Not only that but you may not even experience anything that resembles any of the mentioned experiences that are said to be various levels that can be reached, this could be because of work already done by yourself in previous existences and because of many other factors on top of those mentioned previously. So someone can be at a deeper level of meditation or spiritual level without experiencing some of the less deep stages on the way. And trying and wanting to reach a certain level or experience almost guarantees that you won't experience or reach it, such is the subtle difficulty of meditation.

On a beginning level of meditating, I would find sometimes that if a sound be heard, that sound would translate into shapes seen by my eyes on the back of my eyelids, perhaps a sharp sound would be what looks like a jagged line like the warning symbol for electricity, other sounds could be any shape, sometimes even a sound would suddenly bring a whole colour picture to my mind, so fast that I couldn't really make out what the picture was of. I would continue to place my concentration on the breath without holding it, and let go of any thoughts until I didn't even notice the in and out of breathing falling further into a deeper state of meditation. I know I'm not enlightened, but I did have an experience that was showing something of the immense power the Buddha had as a being.

I attended a meditation and study evening with a group that belonged to a Tibetan Buddhist lineage in Windsor. Part of the evening they read from a book telling stories from acts the Buddha had done in previous incarnations before becoming the last Buddha. This particular story was of a time when the Buddha belonged to a small fishing village. Forgive me for the inaccuracy of the retelling of the story here, but the information is close enough for our purpose. For some reason all the villagers became ill, from some kind of poisoning and they needed to be fed fish in order to survive. Unfortunately the fish also were all dead due to this poisoning, only a very few survived. The Buddha was one of the villagers that was gravely ill, and in fact had passed away. But as the Buddha was passing away he pulled back from passing into Nibbana and brought himself back as a fish, so that someone could eat him and survive. He did this not once, but thousands of times, until the village was saved. This was a story showing the compassion and love the Buddha felt for humanity and his level of commitment to help deliver people from suffering. Someone read out the story out aloud and then we were put into small groups and asked to write down our thoughts on the story and tell the others at the end.

What happened to me whilst this story was being told, is that when the Buddha was stopping himself from passing into Nibbana, I could actually see the light of Nibbana and feel the strength of the pull from its power pulling the Buddha towards it. It was an amazing intense feeling, and I knew that this was the gateway to going *home* and could literally *feel* the powerful pull to go into it. I knew that if it was me, I would be gone in a nano-second, to resist that pull would have been absolutely impossible. But then the Buddha did not resist this incredible pull once, he did it *thousands* of times. The feeling was overwhelming I knew that the light and pull was of something, somewhere I needed to get to. But more than that I knew that whatever being the Buddha was, he was no man, certainly no ordinary man, he may have lived in the physical body of a man, but the being that resided within was so powerful that it was unrecognisable as an ordinary man. I realised just *how* far away I was from this magnificent being, and that it seemed like an impossible quest to reach that state. I just *knew* that I, myself, was thousands of lives away from being a Buddha. But still, this vision and experience was a gift, I felt privileged to have been given such an insight, perhaps an encouragement to work hard and to give me the understanding of how much effort was needed to achieve my chosen task, one that would mean spending all of my waking time to the practice of awakening.

Still, I carried on meditating, because I knew that if it was true that I was stuck in the cycle of birth and death, and the only escape was through reaching Nibbana, I had better get on with it, as there was a *long* way to go! One of the reasons I felt like life was prison, one which I needed to escape from, can be summed up by an experience I had as a schoolboy.

I must have been 14 or 15 yrs old now, a couple of years after my experience with the UFO, and lots of experiences I had undergone already. I hated school, for various reasons, apart from being at one of the roughest in the area. Life was just *not* enjoyable and on top of that I kept having déjà vu experiences. There was one that was to cement my belief that I was in a prison, one of which I needed to escape. I would be travelling to school on the bus, and as I passed through the village of Ash in Hampshire, I noticed someone from out of the window getting into his car to go to work, a cyclist would pass and skid on the pavement right behind the car. Now sometimes the morning bus would be a double decker and sometimes it would be a single decker bus. But for this incident I was travelling on a double decker, and I would be looking down from a seat roughly in the middle of the bus. I noticed this incident, and thought very little of it, I carried on with the grey trudge of school life at the beginning of the week. The next day I was on the bus and sure enough, as I was looking out the window again on the way to school, I saw the same incident. One could surmise that I always went to school at the same time, and that people would go to work, also at the same time every day, a routine, but, this was *the same* incident. I couldn't believe at the exact same time, the exact same incident and skid of the bike, when the bus was passing at the very same point and I was looking out the window in the very same way, the very same time, could it be a *coincidence*!? No, this was déjà vu, I had seen it before, was it one of those dreams of the future? or was it a re-living of the same moment. I soon forgot about it as the day took my attention away. The next morning on the bus, yes, the very same incident, *again,* not only that, but it seemed that it happened maybe 5 times. I could definitely recall 3 times, but it was surely more. A very powerful feeling and emotion came over me, it was not a nice feeling, and it hit me in the pit of my stomach. "Oh my god" I thought, "I'm re-living the same day over and over again. Does that mean I'm stuck in the same day? there's no way out, because my memory does not kick in until the exact moment when I see that déjà vu moment on the bus". It's like I must wake up every day with my memory wiped and just start the same day over again. Maybe it's not the day, maybe it's the week. The thought of spending eternity going to a school and life you hate had a devastating and powerful effect. Then life all of sudden seemed like a prison, one a person was stuck in, chained, like the prisoners in Plato's cave, watching the shadows on the wall opposite and thinking that was life, and not seeing they are chained together to a wall in a cave. As soon as I had this feeling of being imprisoned, all one could do, was try to think of a way of escaping, of getting out from this hell. I thought that I needed to stay alert, stay very awake, to notice everything, there must be a way of escaping, maybe by trying to do something different, to break the cycle.

That was to make my search for answers and plans to escape a strong one, so when I had the experience of seeing the Buddha's resolve and compassion to come back many thousands of times to help the people, it had a very great effect. But here was the path to home, the escape plan. I needed to become enlightened. I was to find out that the Buddha was an exceptional being, one that appears only at a time when the teaching has gone and needs to be re-invented, which according to the scriptures was after 5,000 years had passed, now being roughly 2,500 years so only half way. Also that a person does not need to become a Buddha in order to escape the cycle of birth and death, one needs only to become enlightened. And the Buddha taught that everyone had the possibility of enlightenment and there was a great many enlightened beings when the Buddha was teaching, made possible through his teaching. These people that had achieved enlightenment through his teaching were called Arahants.

I found that this is possible in one lifetime, if all the conditions were right for a person through their actions and good deeds, and through efforts given in previous lives. So enlightenment *is* attainable, and I was to feel it as a definite possibility, which ultimately led me to the monastery. Enlightenment is not something however that is *gained*, it is something that is a natural part of *all* of us, we only need to *realise* it. I had many Meditational experiences and got deeper and deeper through a lot of practice. At one time it was as though I would almost disappear entirely. I would get to a place where there was nothing, no-thing, so empty was this space that there was not even a recollection or feeling of oneself. No senses or thoughts, nothing. Then, there was a sound, and the experience could be explained like this:

'Imagine that you are in a cave, so dark and so quiet that you have lost yourself, or any idea or semblance of yourself, in fact, you do not exist at all. But, that you are on the edge of a great lake of water in this great cave. The water is so still, that you are completely unaware of its presence, as there is no sound or feeling of it at all. But then, there is a sound, it is like someone has thrown a pebble into the great lake. Now that pebble has made waves, ripples in the water. Now that there was a sound, you become aware that there is sound, and then slowly as the ripples spread out, touching other sides of the lake the other senses return. And now you are aware of yourself again, aware of the consciousness, being aware of sound. Now you are aware of consciousness being aware of all the senses of feeling. Then you become aware of the fact that until that moment of sound returning, there was no consciousness, and therefore no senses, because they are attached to the consciousness, it was as though the lake was consciousness. And before it was disturbed there was only awareness.'

Such is the difficulty of putting spiritual experiences into words, which is why the Buddha never talked directly about enlightenment, but only encouraged everyone to practice, and to know by directly experiencing enlightenment themselves.

19.Empathy and Telepathy

Meditation expands the mind and your awareness of what goes on in your mind and your everyday life. Most practitioners of meditation see a lot of changes in themselves, perhaps just in their own character, by being calmer, not to anger so easily, and being able concentrate better. But there are more abilities that are enhanced by meditation, some which are not spoken about so freely, due to the resistance of science and society to their implications. Also to the very limiting by modern science to anything that contradicts or challenges the current accepted wisdom. Even the Buddhist monks will not talk openly about these things, mainly due to something that happened in the time when the Buddha was still alive. Some monks used the extraordinary abilities they gained through practise to show off to locals, in order to gain favour and get more food and be treated like royalty. This led to other monks and those pretending to be monks to lie and cheat about their abilities in order to also gain favour. The Buddha looked down on such behaviour, and in order to stop imposters and Monks from abusing their position and power he banned the use of such showmanship to curry favour. He also ordered that any monk who implies or openly states to have such and such gift, but without actually possessing such and such gift would be disrobed, and no longer a monk immediately, banned for his life from returning to the robes. So now monks are scared of even suggesting any gifts or abilities, in case they haven't really, in case they are no longer a monk for saying it.

But the truth is many monks and lay people have developed abilities that seem amazing, as I had found out in my travels, and from my own experience. I found that as my meditation developed, I first began to be more aware of myself. Then as it developed more, my awareness grew out from myself to those around me, so that I started to be more aware of what other people were experiencing and feeling.

I found that I could *feel* the emotions of others, it generally had to be a strong emotion, but I knew of others that felt almost all emotions of others all the time. One time I was in the Sala of the monastery and sitting quietly at the back at lunchtime waiting for the lunchtime ceremonies to begin. Then I suddenly came over with the most terrible feeling of loss, grief, as though someone close had died. I sat with it and wondered why, and perhaps who was feeling such a pain. The ceremony started and the senior monk read out notes left for him. Congratulations on someone's birthday, good luck for someone's exams, and then condolences to a lady near the front for the loss of her brother who recently passed away due to a motor accident. At the mention of this the woman burst into tears and immediately I knew that those feeling of grief I felt were hers. Not just because she started to cry, but just a kind of *knowing* that it was her. It was not always like this though, sometimes I could be in a group of several people at work. I came over with the feeling of loss, like your partner had left you, and you have that empty feeling in the pit of your stomach, like part of you has been torn out. But *who* was feeling this? With the normal British 'stiff upper lip' and refusal to show emotion, whoever it was, was hiding it well. So it just was not possible to know who it was. I just had to suffer the feeling, and wait for it to subside, because even though it came on quickly, once in, it takes time for the feeling to move on.

This reminded me of an experience I had soon after I was ordained as a novice at the monastery. One day I felt the need to see and talk with someone. I wandered around to see the normal people I would talk to, but none could be found. I started to feel rather lonely, and realised that there was a horrible feeling of loneliness coming over me, so I went back to my room and picked up a book to read to try and escape the feeling. But then when I realised that I was trying to escape this terrible lonely feeling, the words of my mentor started to ring in my ears, that this "was a golden opportunity, to understand yourself". So I put the book down and just sat there, sat with the feeling and let it take over me. Then I tried to understand it, to understand *why* I felt this way, and what caused it?

As I sat there I realised that I put a lot of store in other people, I put my safety or escape in the fact that someone was always there to talk to, when I felt lonely or needed someone to help take the feelings away. I put, as they explained in the monastery, my *center* in something outside of myself. I was taught that one needs to find the center in one's self, the place of calm when all about is a storm, is a place within one's self. If when meditating or meditate walking, and I felt centred, it's a place in my solar plexus where I felt this feeling. I realised that *I* needed to *be* the center, that I had placed my center in others. So when I felt that loneliness I immediately went out to look for solace in another person, but because I couldn't find anyone I felt lost. So I needed to make myself the center for when I needed it and not outside of myself. Because everything is subject to change, and is impermanent, it's not always there when you need it if you put your center *outside* of yourself, but it is always there if the center is ***within yourself***. So I sat there and realised why I had this loneliness, because I had my center outside of myself. I sat there and watched this feeling, as it didn't have the same effect on me now I knew how it came about. The interesting thing is that I saw it, and watched this *feeling, emotion* and watched it as it slowly went away. Now I saw it from a different perspective, it was like a separate entity to myself. I knew why I had felt lonely, so why was it still there? The effect was lessened but still it was there. I watched it with great interest as it slowly went away. It was like a ***thing*** a ***separate*** thing to myself, I felt it, and it was effecting me internally, but it was ***not me***, That's right, it was not me. I didn't own it. So emotions are something we let in to ourselves, due to some reason, but they are not ours, they do not belong to us, but just visit us and are let in by some means. In this case the loneliness was let in by the fact that I had put my center in others and not myself. This had allowed that emotion to come in, and even though once I knew what and why I felt that way, I had to wait for the emotion to go of its *own* accord. So I watched it leave, astonished at the realisation of what had just happened. We believe in our emotions so much, believing that they *are* us. We even *identify* ourselves with the emotions, like *I am* Lonely, or *I am* angry, but truth is, we are *not,* we are just identifying ourselves with it, so that we *become* it, we become Lonely or we become angry. Once you see and *realise* that, their power over you is reduced massively. What a revelation, but the repercussions for this were wide. So now I was able to become even calmer and not so angry, I didn't get affected so much by almost anything anymore, because I knew the reality of emotions and was much more prepared for them. I could still get angry or sad etc of course, these things can catch you unawares, I didn't become a feelingless automaton but because of my *realisation* of the nature of emotions life was a lot different.

After this I became not only more aware of my own emotions but then more aware of other people's emotions too. It was after this I started to feel others emotions. Exactly why that should be is still a mystery to me, but perhaps simply by understanding something at a deeper level gives you the ability to experience it at a deeper level, including when others are feeling it. Because, also, when I felt emotions, either watching a sad movie or listening to music that I enjoyed, I feel the emotion *much deeper* than ever before, the experience of it is heightened. So now I cry much more easily at things like sad movies, and feel much *more* than before. But on the flip side, if something is happening in my life which could upset me, like a break up of a relationship, I am much less affected, and can stand at an emotional distance from it and not be caught up in the suffering that I would once be subject to. So my control over being affected by emotions was much greater, So now I had empathy with others, and was able, if the emotion was strong, to feel it, at a distance, but normally only if they are in the area. But when I was seeing someone in a relationship and they wanted to break off with me, or had broken off in their hearts. I could literally *feel* it. And it would be literally in my heart that it would be felt, if I had a strong connection with them. Or it could be from the stomach. So even if they had not told me yet, I could know. So there is some connection with all beings that is constant and can be felt at any distance.

There was occasion also when I would know what someone was thinking, I had some experience with this before the monastery, but again after my time there and intensive meditation, it was heightened. my experience of knowing what people were thinking was also not all the time but only rarely, and I have no seeming control over it. But the way it presents itself, was not literally *hearing* the voice of someone else in my head or theirs, but was like someone had *told* me *before* what they were thinking, but, that I had forgotten and now was retrieving the memory of what they said. So I didn't hear them speaking, but just my own mind repeating back, but not really in words either, it is more just a *knowing* of what was thought. If you remember my experience with the monk that could read minds, the monk *knew* what I was thinking, but the monk could not understand a word of English. So he could not have heard my thoughts, but could only have *known* what I was thinking. So you see, there must be a *universal* language that is used by *all* minds to transfer information and understanding. It could not be words, but more by *feeling*.

In The case of the abduction scenario with aliens, mostly people say that there was communication with aliens but it was telepathic in nature. This would also lend support to the notion of a *universal* plane of consciousness shared by all, whereby language is

83

transcended and unnecessary. It would also explain why the contact was telepathic.

Another time I was helping a friend out with making a wooden fence around a field for a customer. We were in need of more wood for making this rustic fence, and so set off into a copse which adjoins the field in which we were working to look for a suitable small tree or branches. As we traipsed through the woods we had cause to step over some fallen small trees. One of these trees was at a steep angle to the ground and I had to rest my hand upon the tree to step over it. When I touched the tree I had the most amazing feeling, it was like I could *feel* that the tree was dead. It may seem like an obvious thing on first glance that the tree having fallen was dead, but it *could* have still been alive and recently fallen. But it was more than that, information was passed from the tree to myself, and it was the ***feeling*** of death. It shocked me so much that I snatched my hand up quickly with a start. Then I looked around and felt that the forest was ***alive.*** Of course the forest *was* alive, but this was in a sense that we don't normally perceive forests or plants to be alive. It was now like I knew that the tree had some kind of consciousness, that although they couldn't communicate with us in a language that we normally understand, they did have ***something*** that was communicable by touch, presumably if the person touching had the openness of their senses to receive the information.

Years after this experience when I was at the monastery, there was a wood that belonged to the monastery and a lot of the trees were felled to make way for more planting or some other reason deemed necessary. And when walking into the woods I felt like I could feel the lost spirits of trees rushing around feeling lost. This was hard to put into any known context, and was confusing. It was never the less how I felt in those woods for some days after, until I felt them no more. The Buddhist scriptures had mention of guardians of the trees or spirits that lived in them. And although despite my many experiences my natural nature in fact is scepticism, and thought this was some flight of fancy or romantic notions by some Buddhist scholar. But my experience again leads me to question my own scepticism and I decided that *perhaps* there was more to it than I thought.

So how far does this interconnection with all things in the universe go? What is also possible or not possible? Could it be dangerous, and if so, how dangerous could it be? Another experience I had whilst at school may show how the mind could be a dangerous weapon. I was perhaps 15 years old at the time and attending a physics class. I was doing an experiment with my friend Keith, using a Bunsen burner. There was one of the schools bullies in this class, and he was doing the rounds of the classroom ruining other pupils physics experiments. He got to mine and Keith's experiment burned whatever liquid was being used for the experiment thus rendering it useless. Keith decided that this was just not on and shouted to the class teacher what had happened. This of course did not go down well with the bully and he said in no uncertain terms that he was going to get us both after class. This was no idle threat and we were certainly both 'for it'. Keith panicked a lot at this and at the end of class refused to go out and told the teacher of the threat made by the bully. So the teacher called back into class the bully and let us go whilst talking to the bully. This was only to anger the bully even more and he said to us on the way back into the class that he was going to kill us now! the threat became a much more real threat than just the good kicking we might have received otherwise. So this was a Friday and we left for home for the weekend. I lived a good 5 miles from school by bus and had no connection with schoolmates at evenings or weekends. I was really scared by the threat and worried constantly about it. So much so that I took to wishing the bully dead. So in my head I would repeat over and over again, that the bully would be killed. I really **meant** *it* and this is the important factor that I even **believed** that I **could** wish his death. I would do this the whole weekend, but on Sunday for some reason I changed his mind and didn't want to be the reason for someone's death and changed the mantra to not killed but injured so badly that he could not carry out his threat.

The weekend came to an end and even though I thought of not going to school to avoid the possible repercussions, I went anyway. On the way from the bus stop to school I saw Keith. But Keith was happy and smiling and not looking like he had a care in the world. I asked him, why was he so happy, was he not worried about the bully that was after us? Keith replied "haven't you heard?", "No", I said, Keith went on describe how the bully had been knocked down by a car on Saturday, everyone thought he was going to die, and he was in a coma, but then on the Sunday to everyone's surprise he remarkably came round from his coma. He was in no state to come back to school and would spend some months away, but he would live.

Remarkable all right, I couldn't believe it, it was **exactly** as I had wished. Not only had he been possibly killed and in a coma on the Saturday, but when I changed my mantra on the Sunday for him not to die but just to be incapacitated enough not carry out his threat, he remarkably came out of his coma. This was perhaps too much of a coincidence for me to believe. But could it be true? Was I the reason for this accident, could I have affected the world so directly? It no doubt would be considered a coincidence by many, but I was convinced I had a hand in it. So this is a warning, that if you do think you have an ability, then one should be careful to use it for good and not for harm or through fear, as I felt guilty about this event for quite some time, but it did make me feel more aware of my responsibility to others and to the power of what the mind is capable of.

There are also reports of tests by the Russians of people being able to stop the heart of an animal at a distance as a sort of psychic assassination. The limits of what a person is capable of is unknown and there are many things I am sure that the ruling scientific and government agencies don't want people to know. Perhaps some of what is hidden is actually hidden for a good reason.

Even the Buddha maintains the possibility of a person who has trained their mind to a high degree can affect the *materialistic* world:

AN 6.41

PTS: A iii 340

Daruka-khandha Sutta: The Wood Pile

It has been said that on one occasion the Blessed One (The Buddha) was staying near Rajagaha on Vulture's Peak Mountain. Ven. Sariputta put on his robes and carrying his bowl and outer robe came down from Vulture's Peak Mountain early one morning with a large group of monks, when he saw a large wood pile off to one side. He said to the monks, "Brothers, do you see that large wood pile over there?"

"Yes, Brother," the monks replied.

"Friends, if he wanted to, a monk with psychic power, having attained mastery of his mind, could will that wood pile to be nothing but earth. Why is that? There is earth-property[1] in that wood pile, in dependence on which he could will that wood pile to be nothing but earth.

"If he wanted to, a monk with psychic power, having attained mastery of his mind, could will that wood pile to be nothing but water... fire... wind... beautiful... unattractive. Why is that? There is the property of the unattractive in that wood pile, in dependence on which he could will that wood pile to be nothing but unattractive."Note

1. Or: earth-potential.

("Daruka-khandha Sutta: The Wood Pile" (AN 6.41)

abhiñña *[abhi~n~naa]*:

> Intuitive powers that come from the practice of concentration: the ability to display psychic powers, clairvoyance, clairaudience, the ability to know the thoughts of others, recollection of past lifetimes, and the knowledge that does away with mental effluents.

I think in modern quantum physics this is borne out by revealing that *everything* is made of basically the same thing, which means that everything could have the *potential* of being anything else, if there was a means by which we could manipulate things at their quantum level. Perhaps we have those means, by our very own minds, using concentration, will and belief?

20.Windows to another dimension

After disrobing as a Novice monk, I set off to a town called Gillingham in the county of Kent in South East England. I had some friends there and a room in which to stay. On the morning of leaving the monastery I was heading out on a road towards the M25 which circles London, and in the half light of the early morning I saw above roughly where the town Watford is in north London a strange but familiar sight of what can only be described as a UFO. It was kind of oval shaped, but was a mixture of colours, orange and white lights. Kind of oval because it appeared to be changing shape from oval to round and the colours were moving also. I looked and was kind of happy to see it, it *felt* friendly, perhaps because of the distance away, or maybe I was getting used to seeing such odd sights? I felt also maybe it was some kind of sign, as it was the very day I left the monastery back to Lay life, I hoped it was a good sign as I said "hello" in my mind as it disappeared from sight as I drove around the roads.

Earlier on in this book I told of my strange experience with the moon when driving to work early in the morning. I had asked Eduardo my friend from the monastery who is now a Monk and now has a Pali name 'Dhammiko' and as this is being written has gone to live in Thailand for several years. Dhammiko is well versed in astrology and astronomy and I asked him if there was any astronomical reason why the moon would seem to be in such different parts of the sky just 2 nights apart? Dhammiko's response was that there was no way the moon could possibly have behaved in such a manner, and that whatever I saw it most certainly could *not* have been the moon. Immediately in my mind came the notion of a UFO. It meant that this UFO would have to have been absolutely *massive* as it was giving the impression of the size and luminosity of the moon. But as stated earlier, I still believe it was the moon because although it shouldn't have been in that part of the sky, it was in actual fact the *only* large moon like object in the sky. If it was not the moon, then the moon was even more mysterious by its complete absence! It was a clear night and could not have been hidden by any cloud cover. So was it a UFO mistaken by Me on that morning, or the misplaced moon, or in fact could it be something to do with the area in which I witnessed this event?

On another morning as I was going to work again at around 4am I was driving from Gillingham to Aylesford using the A229 which comes out of Chatham and rises up and down in an area known as Blue Bell Hill. As I was cresting and about to drive down Blue Bell Hill I saw a UFO over what looked like the Maidstone area in front of me. I instantly recognised this UFO as the same type of one that I saw on the morning leaving the monastery it was the shape changing orange and white. Could it in fact be the same one? Perhaps the same people even keeping an eye on me and letting me know? So now 2 strange events in the morning on the way to work, I was still driving through Chatham when noticing the moon displacement on that earlier event but going in the same direction as I always did on the way to work.

I was reading the fortean times magazine and to my surprise read a ghost story about Blue Bell Hill, this lead me to investigate the area in more depth.

I discovered that Kent is the oldest recorded county name in Britain (both the Romans and Greeks referred to it as Kention, and its populace Canti), Kent is also called the Garden of England - a nod to the legendary hop fields and orchards scattered across the countryside. Kent's 1900 square kilometres is home to rolling hills, villages, coastal towns, and atmospheric marshland; the vicinity around the Downs is now recognised as an Area of Outstanding Natural Beauty. The age and deep history of the area is no doubt why there are countless ghost stories about the county. Indeed the village of Pluckley is said to be the most haunted village in England, and maybe even the world, in a country that is said to be the most haunted in the world that's quite a statement!

But Neil Arnold who has recently published a book called *Paranormal Kent* has stated that "Blue Bell Hill is, I believe, the most haunted place in Britain," (http://www.monstrous.com/Monstrous_Literature/Paranormal_Kent_by_Neil_Arnold.html)

Blue Bell Hill has a history as long as the rest of Kent and even stranger than most due to the diverse amount of phenomena witnessed. We will start with the ghost stories.

http://www.roadghosts.com/blue%20bell%20hill.htm

"GHOST GIRL SEEN AGAIN"

So ran the front page headline of the Kent Today of Tuesday 10 November 1992.

The article, by Emma Cooper, described the 'chilling new turn' in the saga of Kent's most famous phantom. The incident, it was reported, had taken place 'around midnight' the previous Sunday night (8 November) near the Aylesford turn-off of the southbound carriageway of the A229 at Blue Bell Hill, some four miles to the north of Maidstone.

Ian Sharpe, a 54-year-old coach driver, was on the last leg of his journey home to Maidstone when a young woman had appeared in the path of his vehicle, ran towards him and, with her eyes locked on his, fallen beneath the bonnet. Horrified, Ian skidded the car to a halt, and shakily got out to take account of the accident.

"I honestly thought I had killed her," he said. "You can't imagine how it felt. I was so scared to look underneath, but I knelt down and looked straight through - there was nothing there."[1]

Ian searched around about the car, and in the bushes of the wide verge, but found nothing. Attempts to flag down two cars for assistance failed, so he continued on into Maidstone, making straight for the police station to report the incident.

White-faced and 'shaking like a leaf', he told police that he had run over a woman but could not find the body. After listening to Ian's account, in course noting the particular spot on Blue Bell Hill where the incident had occurred, the police seemingly came to an immediate if presumptuous judgment by recounting to him the 'spooky legend' of the ghost said to haunt that stretch of road.

Nevertheless, officers accompanied him back to the scene, and a search of the area ensued, which proved fruitless. No sign of damage was found on his car, reinforcing opinion that he could not have encountered a real person. But Ian maintained, he had not been 'seeing things'. The girl had seemed perfectly real, not as he imagined a ghost would be.

The following day, Ian Sharpe was said to still be expecting the police to knock at his door to report the finding of the girl's body. It had been, he said, the 'most scary' experience of his life.

This is just one of many stories about the road here is another: http://www.creepybritain.co.uk/xfiles/paranormal-actvity/england/kent/the-phantom-hitch-hiker-of-blue-bell-hill.html

Blue Bell Hill's most famous ghost is that of a female phantom hitch-hiker who has been witnessed by many motorists driving along the A229, many of whom have either stopped to pick her up or worse still run her over.

The haunting started soon after a tragic road accident which occurred on the A229 late one Friday evening on the 19th

November 1965. Four young women were travelling in a Ford Cortina heading towards Maidstone when their car collided with a Jaguar coming in the opposite direction. One of the girls who was to be married the next day died instantly and two of the other shortly after, the fourth girl although badly injured survived.

Shortly after this horrific accident reports started to come in of the ghost of a woman hitching a lift along the road, trying to get to Maidstone.

In 1974 one man reported that he had been driving home late one night when he knocked over a young girl who was walking in the road. Stopping his car the man ran back along the road and picked up the girl who he said was badly bruised and very distressed. He tried to flag down passing motorists but no one would stop so he wrapped the girl up in blankets and laid her on the back seat of his car and drove to the nearest police station. When he stopped the car the girl had vanished.

The next morning police and sniffer dogs searched the area in vain trying to find the young girl but no trace of her was ever found.

In 1992 a man reported that he was driving down Blue Bell hill when a young woman ran out into the road in front of him, he said that she looked at him straight in the eye before she disappeared beneath the bonnet of his car. The poor man screeched his car to a halt and searched the road for her body, he found nothing and very shaken he drove to Maidstone Police station to report the accident. Again despite searches of the area no trace was found.

Similar sightings continue on a regular basis to this day with drivers stopping to give the woman a lift only to find that she disappears or spotting her on the road.

Sometimes the hitch-hiker is a young woman, sometimes a young girl and on occasions she's been described as an elderly woman.

It has been mentioned that the ghostly apparitions are seen whenever there is some major roadwork's such as to the M20 which runs over the A229, so perhaps that disturbs a latent energy to the place which then reveals itself as strange apparitions?

It turns out that ghosts are not the only Phenomena to be found there as evidently a terrifying hag-like apparition was seen by a family of 5 on the hill back in 1993. There has also been spotted a 'white dog' and in the 16th century a ghost hound. The 'beast of Blue Bell hill is evidently a large black cat as has been spotted twice by Neil Arnold himself. Then we see that a red-eyed bipedal humanoid first reported around the neighbouring village of Wouldham during the 1900's was witnessed.

Also in the neighbouring area many other strange phenomena and creatures have been witnessed, such as a huge eel like creature that lived in the depths of the Medway river. Then in 2007 a 30ft long beast was seen swimming in the Medway River near Rochester Bridge.

In 1966 in Chatham a Mr Chester was awoken by his daughter claiming that her sister was missing from her bed, the family searched in vain for the girl and all the doors and windows were locked so she could not have gotten out. Mr Chester decided to phone the police from a local telephone box, but as he got to the Telephone box he heard a voice in his ear telling him 'we have returned her'. He then rushed home to find her in the bed in which she was missing from earlier rubbing her eyes as if she had been asleep all along.

The A229 road that goes from Maidstone to Chatham is in fact an ancient Roman road, which shows it has history, but the history is even older as Just off the A229 on Blue Bell Hill is

Kit's Coty, which is the name of the remains of a Neolithic chambered long barrow which is dated to between 4300 and 3000 BC, and is one of the best known megaliths in Britain. The tallest stone of which is 8 feet (2.4 meters) high and the capstone 4 by 2.7 meters, which was once covered by an earthen mound of 180 feet (55 meters) long, as aerial photographs, have shown. Side ditches were once up to 3.8 meters deep. This site was already famous in the seventeenth century. Samuel Pepys the famous diarist described it as:

"Three great stones standing upright and a great round one lying on them, of great bigness, although not so big as those on Salisbury Plain. But certainly it is a thing of great antiquity, and I am mightily glad to see it."

A large stone shown in the sketch below by Stukely in 1722 and known as 'the General's Tomb', was blown up in 1867. The large mound, also visible on that sketch, has also all but vanished.

'coty' means the same as 'house'. The story explaining the name tells us that Kit is Catigern, who, together with his brother Vortimer fought Hengist and his brother Horsa here around 455, which is recorded both in the *Historia Brittonum* as well as in the *Anglo-Saxon Chronicle.*

Across the road is another neolithic chambered tomb, or rather the sorry remains of it. It was once also a burial chamber, but today the stones are a confused tumble. This is Little (or Lower) Kit's Coty House (TQ 744604), also called the Countless Stones because it is one of those megaliths whose stones can supposedly never be counted twice.

To top things off, this place is evidently also haunted; ghostly re-enactments of a (this?) battle are said to have taken place at one time or another. Another tradition is that at full moon you may place a personal object on the capstone, walk around the dolmen three times, after which the object will have disappeared. I haven't tried it myself though!

Stukely's 1722 sketch

Picture's of Kit's Coty by author 5/02/2011

Map with pin showing where Kit's Coty is situated.

This all says to me that the area is steeped in history, as people for thousands of years have had an interest and respect for the area. Perhaps this is one of the *'Window'* areas where time, space, parallel universes and other dimensions come close to each other, perhaps making it possible or easier for Those ET's from other dimensions to cross over? Or perhaps it's an area of great energy that attracts the UFO's for possible topping up of their power which drives or allows their technology to function. Which is possibly also what attracts or allows the crossover for all the other strange phenomena? As mentioned before by some that the ghosts are seen when road works are going on and the area is disturbed, disturbing the energy field maybe?

The evidence for *window* areas can be found if you look hard enough at reports from areas where there have been regular sightings of UFO's or other anomalous phenomena. Rendlesham Forest for example where the famous UFO landing case mentioned earlier took place, it's also where I myself experienced a very vivid and scary encounter with the otherworldly.

It is not only UFO's that have been witnessed here at Rendlesham Forest but also other phenomena similar to what has been seen at Blue Bell Hill. In the book 'Three men seeking Monsters' by bestselling author Nick Redfern He and two of his friends met an investigator Diane Facer who had spoken to witnesses of creatures prowling the forest. In 1956 Sam Holland was walking his spaniel dog Harry when about 40ft ahead of them they saw a four legged muscular creature with black fur of about 10ft in length. It had a long powerful tail and large claws. The creature apparently seemed to detect the presence of Sam and Harry and stopped in its tracks and turned to look at them. It had a face that seemed like that of a silverback gorilla and a thick neck. It reminded Sam of a creature composed of an Ape a dog, lion and rhinoceros! The creature was apparently not threatened by their presence and strode off after looking at them for about 10 seconds, crashing through the undergrowth indicating it was real and not an apparition. This all took place not more than about 50ft from one of the landing sites of the famous UFO case.

Diane told them of another case from a couple Paul and Jayne Jennings who saw a big black dog in the winter of 1983. The sighting was close to the area of Sam's sighting. They came face to face with a huge hound, but the body was more like that of a feline. It was non-aggressive looking; it even had a 'mournful' look on its face. This time it didn't just saunter off but simply disappeared right in front of them. Then just as shocking it re-appeared and then proceeded to 'flicker' on and off four or five times before permanently vanishing. After which there was a smell of burning metal left in the air. Diane had other tales of strange animals including those with red eyes. And if you remember red eyed bi-pedal beasts as well as large cats were also spotted at Blue Bell Hill. This site has also a very long history like that of Blue Bell hill as there is evidence of Neolithic man dating back to 2500B.C. as mentioned in Nick's book. Also like Blue bell Hill the surrounding area has a history of strange phenomena. For instance there was the tale of the wild man of Orford, below is taken from a website:

http://myths.e2bn.org/mythsandlegends/origins63-the-wild-man-of-orford.html

The Wild Man of Orford

• *Orford Castle*

Wild men are often found in myths, legends and folklore. Some live in snowy or mountain areas, such as the Yeti in the Himalayas, Bigfoot in North America and the Sasquatch in Canada. Other wild men live in the forests, such as the Russian Leshiy, Silenus of Greek mythology and Grendel in the Anglo-Saxon epic, Beowulf.

In many old myths, wild men are violent and frightening. They steal away children and attack humans. However, in other tales, from the late 15th century onwards, the wild men are often gentle beings who look after nature. The wild man of Orford was not violent, just strange and different to the people that captured him.

The wild man of Orford is like many other characters of folklore. He stayed away from people, was big and heavy and very hairy. He had a human face but could only make grunts or cries. Where the wild man of Orford is different, is that he came from the sea and was caught in a fisherman's net. This is why he is sometimes called a Merman.

A Merman is usually a character who is human from the waist up but has a fish's tale, such as Triton in the Greek legends. The Triton had a green beard and hair and played music using a seashell. Another merman, of Norwegian legend, was a monster of huge size that would rise up out of the water. These mermen lived in the sea and were able to

sink ships by calling up great storms. The Wild Man of Orford is sometimes shown in pictures with a fish's tail. Although there is nothing about him having anything fish like, in the first writings about the event, later ones sometimes talk about webbed hands or feet.

• Dungeon in which the wild man was kept

Ralph of Coggeshall wrote down the tale of the Wild Man of Orford, in the Chronicon Anglicanum in 1200, some years after the events. The Cistercian monks at Coggeshall Abbey in Essex kept the document. At this time, Bartholomew de Granvill, As in the story, was kept in the castle. It is likely that a strange man was captured and taken to the castle dungeon and tortured, and he later escaped. However,? who or what he really was, is still a mystery. About the time of the story, people could not decide if this Wild Man was a merman, man, or even an evil spirit that lived in the body of a dead sailor.

Also there is a tale of 'the Black Dog of Bungay' .

The most famous event connected with St Mary's church is the apparition of the devil in the disguise of a Black Dog in 1577. During a storm on Sunday, August 4th, a terrifying thunderstorm occurred with such - 'darkness, rain, hail, thunder and lightning as was never seen the like'.

Storms were always greatly feared during a period when most houses were built of timber and thatch and a lightning strike could quickly set large areas of a town ablaze.

As the people knelt in fear, praying for mercy, suddenly there appeared in their midst a great black Hell Hound. It began tearing around the Church, attacking many of the congregation with its cruel teeth and claws. An old verse records:

'All down the church in midst of fire, the hellish monster flew And, passing onward to the quire, he many people slew'

Then as suddenly as it had appeared, it ran off, departing for Blythburgh Church about twelve miles away where it killed and mauled more people. Bungay Church was damaged, the tower struck by lightening and the Church clock was broken in pieces. Although there is no official record of injuries caused, the Churchwardens account book mentions that two men in the belfry were killed.

Nowadays we would attribute the whole event to the Church having been struck by lightning but, in that superstitious age, many accidents and disasters were considered to be the work of the Devil. There had long been a belief that a Satanic black hound roamed the area and so it was easy to believe for people in the dark interior of the Church, that this evil beast was responsible for the catastrophe.

St Mary's Church still attracts many visitors who come to see where this strange event took place but whereas the door in Blythburgh Church still retains the scorch marks of the Devils claws there is no similar evidence surviving in Bungay.

The Black Dog is sometimes associated with Black Shuck, another spectral hound which haunts the Norfolk and Suffolk coasts. Many people still claim to see these beasts today and a sighting usually results in death or disaster of some kind.

The popularity of the legend has resulted in an image of the Black Dog being incorporated into the Town's coat of arms and there are depictions of him on buildings around the town.

Its name also lives on in the Black Dog Running Club, Black Dog Marathon, Black Dog Antiques and the Black Dogs is the name of Bungay Town Football Club.

(Christopher Reeve)

A ſtraunge,

and terrible *Wunder wrought*
verp late in the pariſh Church
of *Bungay* a *Tovvn of no great di-*
ſtance from the citie of Norwich, name-
ly the fourth of this Auguſt, in ý yeere of
our Lord 1577. in a great tempeſt of violent raine, lightning and thunder, the
like wherof hath been ſel-
dome ſeene.

Wiith the apperance of an horrible ſha-
ped thing, ſenſibly perceiued of the
people then and there
aſſembled.

Drawen into a plain method according to the written coppe.
by Abraham Fleming.

These are two areas that I have experienced the anomalous and both areas have a history of such phenomena, dating back many centuries, and because both also have a recorded history for thousands of years it could be believed that it is because people for thousands of years have also experienced strange phenomena there. There are other parts of the world with similar apparitions and stories such as the skinwalker ranch in Utah USA. I have put an excerpt from Jeff Rense's website below to give an outline of the phenomena happening there:

'Path of the Skinwalker'

A small ranch in northern Utah may be the strangest place on Earth...

By George Knapp November 21, 2002

I'm sitting on a white plastic chair in what seems like total darkness. Strapped to my chest and shoulders is an array of electronic gear--microphones, a video camera, a box that detects magnetic changes and a Geiger counter. Somewhere in the mix is a flashlight, the only device whose function I understand, and thus, the only device I cannot find.

In front of me, I can almost make out the sinister shapes of some truly spooky trees. Malevolent bugs are buzzing in and out of my eyes and ears, and it occurs to me that there must be a tavern open somewhere nearby, even in this remote corner of Utah. One hundred or more yards away, beyond a barbed-wire fence and a little creek, are my fellow paranormal rangers, equipped with their own video cameras, night-vision glasses and assorted scientific gear. They are supposed to be watching me to see if anything happens.

On this night, I am the bait. Bait for what, I wonder? The unspoken hope is my own inherent weirdness quotient might give me some sort of connection to the undeniably odd energy, or entity, that seems to have concentrated itself on this remote rural community, and, in particular, on this small ranch where I now sit, waiting for something to announce its presence.

Some very strange things have happened at the precise spot where I'm sitting. It is here that a visitor was accosted by a roaring but nearly invisible creature, something akin to the Predator of movie fame. It is here that a Ph.D. physicist reported that his mind was invaded, literally taken over, by some sort of hostile intelligence that warned him that he was not welcome. It is here that an entire team of researchers watched in awe as a bright door or portal opened up in the darkness and a large humanoid creature crawled out before quickly vanishing. And it is here that several animals-- cattle and dogs--were mutilated, obliterated or simply disappeared.

For as long as anyone can remember, this part of northeastern Utah has been the site of simply unbelievable paranormal activity. UFOs, Sasquatch, cattle mutilations, psychic manifestations, creatures that aren't found in any zoos or textbooks, poltergeist events. You name it, residents here have seen it.

see below for the rest of the article and more information:

http://www.rense.com/general32/strange.htm

http://en.wikipedia.org/wiki/Skinwalker_Ranch

http://www.skinwalkerranch.org/

21.Continuing UFO interactions

I decided about this time to stop being the hunted/watched and instead to *become* the hunter/watcher and set out to get more solid information and evidence for myself, and to share with others the world over to open people's minds to the larger reality and complexity of our existence. With this end in mind I discovered that a lot of UFO's seemed to use a stealth technology that made them invisible to the human eye but were still visible in the Infrared range of light. Humans are only able to see a very narrow part of the spectrum of light somewhere between the wavelengths of 380 to 750nm as shown in the graph below:

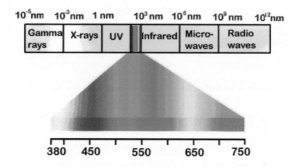

So perhaps it's not hard for a very advanced technological civilization to change the vibration of their craft to emit only in the infrared spectrum which is *just* outside our very narrow perception of light. Or perhaps even, entities and beings live their whole lives in the large spectrum outside of our narrow gaze? Looking for UFO's in the IR spectrum is nothing new though. Possibly the first person to do so was Trevor James Constable, he published a book in 1958 called 'The Cosmic Pulse of Life' a provocative and profound autobiographical book in a quest to understand better the elusive UFO phenomenon, he began using infra-red film in an otherwise ordinary camera. Constable discovered that "Infrared film, exposed between dawn and sunrise in high, dry locales will frequently objectify invisible objects of various kinds living in and passing through the atmosphere." [p.51]

His results were extraordinary. He captured not only conventional discs and spacecraft-like forms on film, but amazing amoeboid entities. Commenting on these, and describing his own astonishment, in his book refers to "...the unwelcome nature of these photographs....These living creatures, these bioforms, were neither what we wanted nor what we expected. We wanted spacecraft. At that time we stood in ignorance of any biological element in UFOs....In the intervening years I have observed with interest and fascination the disquieting, disturbing effect (the photos and film) have on all persons whose approach to UFOs is mechanistic. This experience has taught me that purported scientific "objectivity" is a fiction..." [pp83-4]

I couldn't agree with him more!

Below are a couple of photo's by Trevor James Constable:

So I set about converting my Fuji S5000 digital camera to take pictures in Infrared. This involves taking the camera apart and removing the filter that filters out IR light coming onto the CCD chip. The means to do it are freely available on the internet you just need a few simple tools and some patience. The result is that everything took on a kind of red colour. The other drawback was that focusing was not as sharp once put back together, but it was good enough to test the theory out and do a bit of hunting. The

Fuji S5000 had a video record function and this is what I wanted to use, as I didn't own a video camcorder and was fed up with still photos as people believe less the still photo. But a video is harder to deny in my opinion. On the very *first* outing to see what the video came out like a UFO was captured, unfortunately the screen on the back of the camera is so small that the UFO was only seen when looking back at the footage later on my computer.

It was very brief looked like it was stationary behind a cloud to start.

In this still you can see it's moved its heading away from the camera

The video can be viewed on youtube here:
http://www.youtube.com/watch?v=l9bnsVPagds The footage was taken on the 3rd July 2009.

Then on the next outing to a nearby park where the first UFO was caught, I caught another, or maybe the same UFO? The video was taken on the 12th

July 2009 in exactly the same place as the previous time, but this time went off in a different direction. Although me or my then partner Chari who was with me both times, could not see the UFO with our eyes it looks as though I was following it with the camera. The video can be seen here: http://www.youtube.com/watch?v=gjDxpXJgBO0

Below are some still pictures taken from the video, it is the typical ball of light, but moves very fast under the clouds after again coming from behind a cloud. I had the feeling that it was stationary there and moved once I pointed the camera in its direction. The burning question is, was it there for our benefit and wanted to be seen and filmed. Or was it there watching us not knowing it would be filmed until the camera gave same kind of signature that it could record them/it? The latter seems unlikely, because the UFO could have just disappeared upwards without coming out of the cloud and disappeared into space without ever being seen, instead it shoots off across the observer's field of view *under* the clouds! I believe it could have been a show for me and my partner, as Chari listened to all of my UFO stories but was not necessarily a believer, but after these two incidents she was a bit shocked and unnerved by the reality of it all, or is that just too egotistical to believe that the UFO controllers would do that for us? The other point to note is the location of the recordings. They were in Riverside park Gillingham and on the opposite side of the water is Kingsnorth power station. There were Greenpeace protesters who climbed the large chimney and painted on it in 2007 because the government was considering making the station the countries first *clean* coal burning station. A brief history of events is below taken from Wikipedia:

Six Greenpeace protesters were arrested for breaking in to the power station, climbing the 200 meter chimney, painting the word Gordon on the chimney and causing an estimated £30,000 worth of damage. At their subsequent trial they admitted trying to shut the station down but argued that they were legally justified because they were trying to prevent climate change from causing greater damage to property elsewhere around the world. Evidence was heard from David Cameron's environment adviser Zac Goldsmith, and an Inuit leader from Greenland, both saying that climate change was already seriously affecting life around the world. The six were acquitted after arguing that they were legally justified in their actions to prevent climate change from causing greater damage to property around the world. It was the first case where preventing property damage caused by climate change has been used as part of a "lawful excuse" defense in court.

In December 2008 Greenpeace received a letter from the Crown Prosecution Service revealing that the Attorney-General was close to referring the case of the Kingsnorth Six to the Court of Appeal in an effort to remove the defense of 'lawful excuse' from activists.

Also in December the New York Times listed the acquittal in its annual list of the most influential ideas that will change our lives[.]

As a replacement for the four old Kingsnorth units, in October 2006 EON proposed the construction of two new coal-fired units, Kingsnorth Units 5 and 6. EON currently propose constructing two new 800 MW supercritical coal-fired power units on the site, to be operational "as early as 2012".If completed, this would be the first new coal powered plant in the UK since the completion of the Drax power station in 1986.

EON expects the supercritical units to reduce carbon dioxide emissions per unit of electricity by around 20%, as compared to the existing subcritical plant. EON also says the new units will be "capture ready" to allow the option of retrofitting with carbon capture and storage (CCS). Their environmental statement reads:

"CCS will be considered as an option...subject to the process of CCS being allowed by law and incentivized by a suitable framework and technological hurdles for the process being overcome"

On 31 March 2008 EON announced that the new Kingsnorth power station would be used in a bid for the Government's carbon capture and storage competition. In addition EON proposed that the planning decision should be delayed until after the Government has completed its consultation on CCS.

On 30 June 2008 it was announced that Kingsnorth project had proceeded to the next stage of the competition (prequalification) with three other competitors.

In March 2009 Ed Miliband said that he was postponing a decision on Kingsnorth and then EON chief executive said that "Without commercial carbon capture, it's 'game over'

On 7 October 2009 EON postponed the replacement until at least 2016.

On 20 October 2010 it was announced that the build of the replacement had been shelved.

So at the time of taking those videos the power station change was still a possibility. But UFO's seem predominantly interested in Nuclear energy, such as Rendlesham, when unbeknownst to the general public Nuclear warheads were there in 1980, when all thought they were at Greenham Common. And UFO's have been seen over Nuclear Power stations. Nuclear energy is definitely what interests or more likely *worries* them, so why Kingsnorth? Unless there were, or is, plans to make it a Nuclear Power station? Or something else on the Hoo peninsular was taking their interest. Just further down is St Mary's Island which was originally a marshy area to the north of Chatham Dockyard. It had many uses over the years: brickfields, a prison, and also a place to bury the bodies of the prisoners of war held captive on the prison hulks in the River Medway. But perhaps more intriguingly a place to change the reactor cores of the Royal Navy's submarines, and also a nuclear waste dump. Would you believe that now, after removing 1,300,000 tonnes of contaminated soil, a housing estate! maybe there are still Nuclear remnants in the area or something else more hidden and secretive? Whatever the reason, I caught a UFO twice in the same area coming out from almost exactly the same spot in the sky on the very two occasions I went there to see if I could catch anything on video. I went back to Riverside park and that area many times afterwards taking ten's of video's, but never caught another UFO at that spot, perhaps they thought 'uh oh, we've been rumbled' and decided to move on or to another place, or managed to stay much more hidden? Only you can decide for yourself on the evidence provided.

After this point the UFO seems to disappear into the clouds and I'm turning the camera away from the area as I can't actually see what I've just recorded.

After this initial success I decided to try to catch more daytime UFO's hiding out in the skies, but I needed more equipment so I bought myself a second-hand faulty camcorder from eBay. It was a Sony DCR-SR290 I then bought a 950nm IR (infrared) filter, which only lets through IR light, so that when he turned on the 'Night Shot' function during the day he just needed to screw on the filter which adjusted the exposure level so that the camera could record IR in daylight. The camcorder only cost me £50 as it would not turn on. It was a faulty ribbon cable from the LCD screen to the body of the camera. As I only really used it in the back garden on a tripod I just fiddled with the cable so that it worked and left it recording. This was ok to start and the picture quality was very good. Eventually I sold it on and bought a DCR-SR32 because I wanted a better zoom function. The SR290 had superior picture quality but only a 10x optical zoom, whereas the SR32 had a lesser quality of picture, although still good enough, but had a far greater zoom with 40x optical. I wanted the greater zoom in case I saw a UFO and wanted to zoom in. The results were better and clearer than with the converted Fuji S5000 as you can see by the pictures below, the video in its entirety can be viewed here: http://www.youtube.com/watch?v=JAtMwDfQeyw

The better quality and clarity is immediately obvious, unfortunately the UFO is still just a 'blob' in the sky.

22.Rods

Whilst recording the sky and then looking back through the video footage for UFO's I also started to see another phenomena equally as controversial as the UFO's, This new kind of phenomena are known as ROD's. Originally found and reported by film maker Jose Escamilla, he discovered them in, of all places, Roswell New Mexico where he lived. They appear to be long bodied animals with either a few wings either side of their 'rod' like bodies or a fin like wing. And range in size from a few centimetres to meters long. I have seen something flit by so fast that I couldn't catch exactly what it was but was caught on the video. The presence of these apparently crypto zoological creatures is open to debate, but seems to be something illusive. No one has yet found a 'dead' rod, so one has never been dissected or looked at that closely, and to the sceptics that is enough evidence, or lack of, to conclude their non existence. Could they be another part of the inter-dimensional pantheon of cryptic creatures such as the Big cats, Black dogs or red-eyed bipedal creatures as seen in the 'window' areas mentioned before? It's a possibility I have noticed that when I caught UFO's on video I would almost always see Rod's as well could the two be linked in some way? And also I noticed that they are more visible when recording in IR during the day, so could they be linked with the critters that Trevor J Constable had recorded?

Just as with UFO's the Rods origination is a mystery and the existence or lack of should be determined by none other than you. Simply look at the evidence given and go outside and investigate yourselves, take cameras and camcorders and see if you can capture these illusive phenomena. Then you can make an informed opinion, if you can't find evidence of any of the phenomena mentioned, then that is your result and you can make a decision based on the evidence. And if you do find evidence of the aforementioned phenomena then please join in the army of people already uploading and disseminating their evidence for the education and enjoyment of others. Below are some still pictures of Rods taken from my videos found on YouTube:

Taken from the video which can be seen here:
http://www.youtube.com/watch?v=JAtMwDfQeyw

This Rod was caught later on in the same video as above.

This Rod was caught and can be seen on this video:
http://www.youtube.com/watch?v=vXAH0P1m9_A

23.Conclusions

So what does all this mean? Why are the E.T's so illusive, they give their originality in the stars many light years away, when they say anything about where they are from and yet seem so close in appearance to us, at least a lot of them do at any rate. They remain aloof and distant, and yet seek to see when we are messing with Nuclear energy and give dire warnings of our future to individuals, and are constantly in our skies never seemingly bothered to go home. They abduct people, land and talk to people and fly around in solid objects, yet their craft can disappear as suddenly as they appear, they walk through walls and appear in our dreams. In times past before the 1900's when before even dirigibles were the fashion, that's what people tended to see in the skies or strange shapes with propellers, sometimes they land and ask to borrow ordinary tools, or food or water. But in modern times they are always more advanced in nature. I wonder if this is because they appear within the frame of reference of the observer. I don't believe they need hammers or screwdrivers to fix their craft or the water from farmers wells or food from us. When they are perfectly capable of walking through walls and getting water from places where there are no people and covering the distance of the planet or even galaxy in a few seconds.

What if the reason they give their home address as strange unliveable planets or faraway places or from '*anywhere*' are because all the time they were from right under our noses. They perhaps live *here* not in the three dimensional realm where we move about, but from one of the many dimensions that are right in the space around us all the time. In the living room, the kitchen, the bathroom, the bedroom, right next to you now reading this book, after all our science can only detect a *maximum* of 10% of what is actually here, in the space in the room you are in right now. 90% of reality is invisible to us, that's a lot of unknown reality, what we think of as reality is a tiny percentage of what actually *is*. Some scientists think it may be possible to get from one side of the universe to the other in an instant by using another dimension. Or, think of it this way ... if we hurt our environment here with a Nuclear bomb let's say, (and we don't know the *full* extent of the damage that bomb can do, or has done). We don't know what damage it does to the other realities or dimensions either. And if we can access the whole universe from the space you are sitting in right now, that means the whole of the universe or at least very great distances are connected directly to where you are right now, and therefore could *also* be damaged by that nuclear bomb. This then makes more sense of the odd

UFO's ET's and paranormal experiences

behaviour of the E.T's, that they actually live right here *with* us all the time, even though they could be at great distances from us in *our* 3 dimensional reality. So the reason they are so cagy about where they come from is because they are, in a sense, from right here, and, if we, or at least the military knew that, they would try to exploit it, hunt for them and find ways to root them out to gain their advanced technologies that would undoubtedly then be used against them by our caveman and tribal like behaviour and quest for complete dominance by the military. So in our three dimensional reality they may live very far away, but in the fullness of reality they are right here and also suffer the consequences of our mistakes.

The possibility that our dreams and the *astral* world take place in another dimension, perhaps one that they or at least some of them live in, or are able to access easily may then perhaps answer why my visit from the Men in Black was in my dreams.

Let us take the analogy of a two dimensional being compared to a three dimensional being as a way of thinking about our three dimensional existence compared to beings from higher dimensions. Below has been taken from the book 'TERTIUM ORGANUM. Chapter IV by P.D. Ouspensky'

'Let us next consider the two-dimensional world, and the being living on a plane. The universe of this being will be one great plane. Let us imagine beings on this plane having the shape of points, lines, and flat geometrical figures. The objects and "solids" of that world will have the shape of flat geometrical figures too.

In what manner will a being living on such a plane universe cognize his world? First of all we can affirm that he will not feel the plane upon which he lives. He will not do so because he will feel the objects, i.e., figures which are on this plane. He will feel the lines which limit them, and for this reason he will not feel his plane, for in that case he would not be in a position to discern the lines. The lines will differ from the plane in that they produce sensations; therefore they exist. The plane does not produce sensations; therefore it does not exist. Moving on the plane, the two-dimensional being, feeling no sensations, will declare that nothing now exists. After having encountered some figure, having

117

sensed its lines, he will say that something appeared. But gradually, by a process of reasoning, the two-dimensional being will come to the conclusion that the figures he encounters exist *on something*, or *in something*. Thereupon he may name such a plane (he will not know, indeed, that it is a plane) the "ether." Accordingly he will declare that the "ether" fills all space, but differs in its qualities from "matter." By "matter" he will mean lines. Having come to this conclusion the two-dimensional being will regard all processes as happening in his "ether," i.e., in his space. He will not be in a position to imagine anything outside of this ether, that is, out of his plane. If anything, proceeding out of his plane, comes in contact with his consciousness, then he will either deny it, or regard it as something subjective, the creation of his own imagination; or else he will believe that it is proceeding right on the plane, *in the ether*, as are all other phenomena. Sensing lines only, the plane being will not sense them as we do. *First of all, he will see no angle*. It is extremely easy for us to verify this by experiment. If we will hold before our eyes two matches, inclined one to the other in a horizontal plane, then we shall see one line. To see the angle we shall have *to look*

from above. The two-dimensional being cannot look from above and therefore cannot see the angle. But measuring the distance between the lines of different "solids" of his world, the two-dimensional being will come continually in contact with the angle, and he will regard it as a strange property of the line, which is sometimes manifest and sometimes is not. That is, he will refer the angle to time; he will regard it as a temporary, evanescent phenomenon, a change in the state of a "solid," or as *motion*. It is difficult for us to understand this. It is difficult to imagine how the angle can be regarded as motion. But it must be absolutely so, and cannot be otherwise. If we try to represent to ourselves how the plane being studies

the square, then certainly we shall find that for the plane being the square will be *a moving body*. Let us imagine that the plane being is opposite one of the angles of the square. He does not see the angle-- before him is a line, but a line possessing very curious properties. Approaching this line, the two dimensional being observes that a strange thing is happening to the line. One point remains in the same position, and other points *are withdrawing back* from both sides. We repeat, that the two-dimensional being has no idea of an angle. *Apparently* the line remains the same as it was, yet something is happening to it, without a doubt. The plane being will say that the line is moving, but so rapidly as to be imperceptible to sight. If the plane being goes away from the angle and follows along a side of the square, then the side will become immobile. When he comes to the angle, he will notice *the motion* again. After going around the square several times, he will establish the fact of regular, periodical motions of the line. Quite probably in the mind of the plane being the square will assume the form of a body possessing the property of periodical motions, invisible to the eye, but producing definite physical effects (molecular motion)--or it will remain there as a perception of periodical *moments* of rest and motion in one complex line, and still more probably it will seem to be a *rotating body*. Quite possibly the plane being will regard the angle as his own subjective perception, and will doubt whether any objective reality corresponds to this subjective perception. Nevertheless he will reflect that if there is *action*, yielding to measurement, so must there be the cause of it, consisting in the change of

the state of the line, i.e., in motion. The lines visible to the plane being he may call *matter*, and the angles--*motion*. That is, he may call the broken line with an angle, *moving* matter. And truly to him such a line by reason of its properties will be quite analogous to matter in motion. If a cube were to rest upon the plane upon which the plane being lives, then this cube will not exist for the two-dimensional being, but only the square face of the cube in contact with the plane will exist for him--as a line, with periodical motions. Correspondingly, all other solids lying outside of his plane, in contact with it, or passing through it, will not exist for the plane being. The planes of contact or cross sections of these bodies will alone be sensed. But if these planes or sections move or change, then the two-dimensional being will think, indeed, that the *cause* of the change or motion is in the bodies themselves, i.e., right there on his plane. As has been said, the two-dimensional being will regard the straight lines only as immobile matter; irregular lines and curves will seem to him as moving. So far as *really moving* lines are concerned, that is, lines limiting the cross-sections or planes of contact passing through or moving along the plane, these will be for the two-dimensional being something inconceivable and *incommensurable*. It will be as though there were in them the presence of something independent, depending upon itself only, *animated*. This effect

will proceed from two causes: He can measure the immobile angles and curves, the properties of which the two-dimensional being calls motion, for the reason that they are immobile; moving figures, on the contrary, he cannot measure, because the changes in them will be out of his control. These changes will depend upon the properties *of the whole body* and its motion, and of that whole body the two dimensional being will know only one side or section. Not perceiving the existence of this body, and contemplating the motion pertaining to the sides and sections *he probably will regard them as living beings*. He will affirm that there is something in them which differentiates them from other bodies: vital energy, or even soul. That something will be regarded as inconceivable, and really will be inconceivable to the two-dimensional being, because to him it is the result of an incomprehensible motion of

inconceivable solids. If we imagine an immobile circle upon the plane, then for the two-dimensional being it will appear as a moving line with some very strange and to him inconceivable motions. The two-dimensional being will never see that motion. Perhaps he will call such motion *molecular motion*, i.e., the movement of minutest invisible particles of "matter." Moreover, a circle rotating around an axis passing through its center, for the two-dimensional being will differ in some inconceivable way from the immobile circle. *Both will appear to be moving, but moving differently*. For the two-dimensional being a circle or a square, rotating around its centre, on, account of its double motion will be an inexplicable and incommensurable phenomenon, like *a phenomenon of life* for a modern physicist.

Therefore, for a two-dimensional being, a straight line will be immobile matter; a broken or a curved line--matter in motion; and a moving line--*living* matter. The centre of a circle or a square will be inaccessible to the plane being, just as the centre of a sphere or of a cube made of solid matter is inaccessible to us--and for the two-dimensional being even the idea of a centre will be incomprehensible, since he possesses no idea of a centre. Having no idea of phenomena proceeding outside of the plane--that is, out of his "space"--the plane being will think of all phenomena as proceeding on his plane as has been stated. And all phenomena

which he regards as proceeding on his plane, he will consider as being in causal interdependence *one with another*: that is, he will think that one phenomenon is the effect of another *which has happened right there*, and the cause of a third which will happen right on the same plane. If a multi-colored cube passes through the plane, the plane being will perceive the entire cube and its motion as a change in color of lines lying in the plane. Thus, if a blue line replaces a red one, then the plane being will regard the red line as *a past event*. He will not be in a position to realize the idea that the red line is still existing somewhere. He will say that the line is single, but that it *becomes blue* as a consequence of certain causes of a physical character. If the cube moves backward so that the red line appears again after the blue one, then for the two-dimensional being this will constitute *a new phenomenon*. He will say that the line became red again. For the being living on a plane, everything above and below (if the plane be horizontal), and on the right or left (if the plane be vertical) will be existing in time, in the past and in the future: that which in reality is located outside of the plane will be regarded as non-existent, either as that which is already past, i.e., as something which has disappeared, ceased to be, will never return; or as in the future, i.e., as not

existent, not manifested, as a thing in potentiality. Let us imagine that a wheel with the spokes painted different colors is rotating through the plane upon which the plane being lives. To such a being all the motion of the wheel will appear as a variation of the color of the line of intersection of the wheel and the plane. The plane being will call this variation of the

color of the line a phenomenon, and observing these phenomena he will notice in them a certain succession. He will know that the black line is followed by the white one, the white by the blue, the blue by the red, and so on. If simultaneously with the appearance of the white line some other phenomenon occurs--say the ringing of a bell--the two-dimensional being will say that the white line is the cause of that ringing. The change of the color of the lines, in the opinion of the two-dimensional being, will depend on causes lying right in his plane. Any pre-supposition of the possibility of the existence of causes lying *outside of the plane* he

will characterize as fantastic and entirely unscientific. It will seem so to him because he will never be in a position to represent the wheel to himself, i.e., the parts of the wheel on both sides of the plane. After a rough study of the color of the lines, and knowing the order of their sequence, the plane being, perceiving one of them, say the blue one, will think that the black and the white ones have already passed, i.e., disappeared, ceased to exist, *gone into the past*; and that those lines which have not as yet appeared--the yellow, the green, and so on, and the new white and black ones still to come--do not yet exist, but lie in the future. Therefore, though not conceiving the form of his universe, and regarding it as infinite in all directions,

the plane being will nevertheless involuntarily think of the past as situated somewhere at one side *of all*, and of the future as somewhere at the other side of this totality. In such manner will the plane being conceive of *the idea of time*. We see that this idea arises because the two-dimensional being senses only two out of three dimensions of space; the third dimension he senses only after its effects become manifest upon the plane, and therefore he regards it as something different from the first two dimensions of space, calling it time. Now let us imagine that through the plane upon which the two-dimensional being lives, *two wheels* with

multi-colored spokes are rotating and are rotating in opposite directions. The spokes of one wheel come from above and go below; the spokes of the other come from below and go above. *The plane being will never notice it*. He will never notice that where for one line (which he sees) there lies the past, for another line there lies the future. This thought will never even come into his head, because he will conceive of the past and the future very confusedly, regarding them as concepts, not as actual facts. But at the same time he will be

firmly convinced that the past goes in *one direction*, and the future in another. Therefore

it will seem to him a wild absurdity that on one side something past and *something future* can lie together, and on another side-- and also beside these two--something future and *something past*. To the plane being the idea that some phenomena come whence others go, and vice versa, will seem equally absurd. He will tenaciously think that the future is that wherefrom everything comes, and the past is that whereto everything goes *and where from nothing returns*. He will be totally unable to understand that events may arise from the past just as they do from the future. Thus we see that the plane being will regard the changes of color of the lines lying on the plane very naively. The appearance of *different* spokes he will regard as the change of color of *one and the same line*, and the repeated appearance of the same colored spoke he will regard every time as a *new* appearance of a given color. But

nevertheless, having noticed periodicity in the change of the color of the lines upon the surface, having remembered the order of their appearance, and having learned to define the "time" of the appearance of certain spokes in relation to some other more constant phenomenon, the plane being will be in a position to foretell the change of the line from one color to another. Thereupon he will say that he has *studied* this phenomenon, that he can apply to it "the mathematical method"--can "calculate" it. If we ourselves enter the world of plane beings, then its inhabit-ants will sense the lines limiting the sections of our bodies. These sections will be for them *living beings*; they will not know from whence they appear, why they alter, or whither they disappear in such *a miraculous manner*. So also, the
sections of all our inanimate but moving objects will seem independent living beings.

If the consciousness of a plane being should suspect our existence, and should come into some sort of communion with our consciousness, then to him we would appear as higher, omniscient, possibly omnipotent, but above all incomprehensible beings *of a quite inconceivable category*. We could see his world *just as it is*, and not as it seems to him. We could see the past and the future; could foretell, direct, and even create events. We could know the very substance of things--could know what "matter" (the straight line) is, what
"motion" (the broken line, the curve, the angle) is. We could see an *angle*, and we could see a *centre*. All this would give us an enormous advantage over the two-dimensional being.

In all the phenomena of the world of the two-dimensional being we could see considerably more than he sees--or could see quite other things than he. And we could tell him very much that was new, amazing, and unexpected about the phenomena of his world, provided indeed that he could hear us and *understand us*. First of all we could tell him that what he regards as phenomena--angles and curves, for instance—are *properties* of higher figures; that other "phenomena" of his world are not phenomena, but only "parts" or "sections" of phenomena; that what he calls "solids" are only sections of solids--and many things besides. We would be able to tell him that on both sides of his plane (i.e., of his space or ether) lies infinite space

(which the plane being calls time); and that in this space lie the causes of all his phenomena, and the phenomena themselves, the past as well as the future ones; moreover, we might add that "phenomena" themselves are not something happening and then ceasing to be, but combinations of properties of higher solids. But we should experience considerable difficulty in explaining anything to the plane being; and it would be very difficult for him to understand us. First of all it would be difficult because he would not have the *concepts* corresponding to our concepts. He would lack "necessary words." For instance, "section"--this would be for him a quite new and inconceivable word; then "angle"—again an inconceivable word; "centre"--still more inconceivable; the *third* perpendicular—something incomprehensible, lying outside of his geometry. The fallacy of his conception of time would be the most difficult thing for the plane being to understand. He could never understand that *that which has passed* and *that which is to be* are existing simultaneously on the lines perpendicular to his plane. And he could never conceive the idea that the past is identical with the future, because phenomena come from both sides and go in both directions.'

So what I am proposing, is that perhaps some, not necessarily all, E.T's and UFO's may be from *higher* dimensions. I use the term higher as opposed to different, because as we see from the above interpretation the 3rd dimensional beings 'us' are really from a higher dimension than that of the 2 dimensional being. So any higher dimensional being above our 3 dimensions is able to see 'our' past present and future as one. And therefore sees our whole lives and would be able to interject at any point, presumably. As mentioned by Ouspensky there is a problem of communication with the lower dimensional being. It could also be supposed that, say, if a two dimensional being was able to meditate, and then gain a perspective of the two dimensional realm from an expanded consciousness and seeing the 3rd dimension from outside of his restrictive 2 dimensional mind, he would not have the language or frame of reference to be able to explain it. It could only be experienced by meditating and leaving the confines of the restricted two dimensional mind and reality. So for the two dimensional being to be able to relay his experience of reality to fellow two dimensioners, he would have to encourage them to meditate, as to try and explain in their own language would be impossible or sound totally ridiculous, and even make him look completely mad. He may find some way to approach the feeling of it through analogy or poetry but it still would be incomplete and perhaps misunderstood.

So let's take this analogy further. What if the two dimensioners somehow managed to make a nuclear bomb, the clever little bastards! Now although the bomb was a good weapon in their two dimensional world against other tribes, little did they know that the bomb also had a devastating effect also in the 3rd dimension, making it unstable and causing ripples throughout many dimensions threatening the safety of beings in all the dimensions in that universe. So now the 3 dimensional beings see that action needs to be taken in order for them to stop the proliferation and exploding of these nuclear devices. Perhaps from their standpoint they would like to annihilate the two dimensional beings, but this may be against their moral or lawful code, or perhaps be a last resort, or they wish simply to stop and educate these lower beings and help them to raise their consciousness and understanding. But it could be that they cannot get rid of the two dimensional beings without risking harm to themselves. Two dimensions is inextricably connected to and a part of 3 dimensions, you simply can't have 3 dimensions without the flat surface of the 2 dimensions, it's impossible. If you look at the vast difference in complexity from the 2nd dimension to the 3rd dimension, you can see how vastly more complicated the interaction and consecutiveness is between the 3rd dimension and the higher 4th or 5th dimensions, so trying to do us harm maybe impossible from their point of view, and also points to why what *we* do affects directly any other higher dimension. So they need to find a way to communicate and perhaps to see what is going on along our 3 dimensional world, they could perhaps make devices through their technology that would infiltrate our 3 dimensional world and make them able to see us in our own environment. So now we get to the point of strange UFO's that appear and disappear perhaps into higher dimensions and odd E.T's who seem to do the same and perhaps even abduct people when they are asleep (abduction *in* their sleep), as perhaps the sleeping and astral realms are closer to, or part of, the higher dimensions. People are shown dramatic future visions of cities burning and world collapse as a way to encourage people to live better lives and seek to stop them using the Nuclear energy that is so dangerous to all the dimensions. Also perhaps a lot of the UFO's we see are really E.T. drones perhaps created as spies in the sky in the higher dimensions and sent here to watch and relay back information to the higher dimension beings.

This then can also make some sense of my dream of being chased, with the feeling that there's *nowhere* to hide. As the higher dimensional being would be able to see my whole life and everywhere I could possibly go, so there literally would be nowhere for me to go that would be out of the sight of higher dimensional beings.

I realise that this is far from a complete answer to all anomalies and phenomena, but could hold the answer to the etheric nature and yet apparently solid reality of some UFO's and E.T's. So 'window' areas could simply be portals that are natural or artificially created for the entry and exit of these devises created in other dimensions to come and go. The nature of a portal that leads from one dimension to another may have the added side effect of allowing 'other' dimensions also to seep through, which is the reason for anomalous animals and 'ghosts' also being seen in and around 'window' areas.

I am absolutely sure however, of the existence of advanced technical cultures that are based from, and live, in our three dimensional reality. When one considers the fact that there could be billions of earth like planets in our own galaxy (http://news.bbc.co.uk/1/hi/sci/tech/7891132.stm) in a known universe of **billions** of galaxies the thought of the earth being the only intelligently inhabited planet surely is beyond ridiculous in even the most sceptical of minds.

In an attempt to bring all these diverse experiences and phenomena into one conclusion it has to be noted that we as humans have a vastly incomplete view and understanding of the universe in general. As mentioned above that although we seem separate from the other planets and galaxies across the universe, in the realms of higher dimensions the more these things seem to come together and are part of and not separate from us at all. The start and finish of the life of the two dimensional being as seen from our dimension is one whole, not separated at all, although for the two dimensional being his birth and death seem far apart. The same can be said of us and although we seem separated from our birth and death, they may in fact be part of one whole. Just as we become aware of the fact that we need to live in harmony with our environment in order to survive, we will most likely discover that we also need to live in harmony with the rest of the universe and that things that we do may not just affect our planet, but may affect far beyond.

So the astral realm, ghosts, UFO's and psychic abilities are all varying aspects of the multi-dimensional universe. Some of us seem to have developed a sense for seeing and relating to some part of these higher dimensions, and it seems that contact with the UFO phenomenon can also trigger or open the minds of these witnesses and contactees to then be able to interact with these different parts of reality. This is what the evidence has shown me through personal experience and investigation. There are of course a wide amount of experiences by other people that may point to a different answer, and for sure mis/dis-information put about by governments and others for their own benefit is part of this and as sure as there are people and countries with different agenda's and levels of development. There must also be those same differences and agendas in other cultures and civilisations out in the vast expanses of the universe. If you look at the ancient scriptures of the Hindu's and Sumerians there is evidence of battles in the heavens by what can only be alien cultures, with the idea that the gods that came from the heavens being aliens. But that is another story and there are plenty of writers who have expounded that theory such as Zecharia Sitchin and Erich von Däniken.

So how about the nature of reality? I experienced dreams that became reality and reality that was seen and a part of my dreams. The ability to manipulate dreams consciously and the seeming ability to manipulate reality in the same way, but with a strong concentration and belief in the ability to do so. These things seem separate but are moulding into one another constantly, are in fact dreams and reality then separate at all?

In 1982 at the University of Paris a research team led by physicist Alain Aspect performed what I consider to be one of the most important experiments of the 20th century. Unless you are in the habit of reading scientific journals you probably have never even heard of Aspect's name, but his discovery may have changed the face of science.

Aspect's experiment is related to a consciousness experiment which had been devised by Albert Einstein with Podolsky and Rosen, in order to disprove Quantum Mechanics on the basis of the Pauli Exclusion Principle contradicting Special Relativity.

Aspect and his team discovered that under certain circumstances subatomic particles such as electrons, regardless of the distance separating them, are able to instantaneously communicate with each other. It doesn't matter whether they are 10 inches or 100 billion miles apart.

David Bohm a physicist from the University of London and a former protégé of Einstein's believes Aspect's findings imply that objective reality does not exist, and that despite its apparent solidity the universe is at heart a hologram.

Bohm believes the reason subatomic particles are able to remain in contact with one another regardless of the distance separating them is not because they are sending some sort of signal back and forth, but simply because their separateness is an *illusion*. He argues that at some deeper level of reality such particles are not individual entities, but are actually extensions of the same fundamental thing.

The idea of the Holographic model of the universe became popular and useful to other scientists and helped to shed light on previously unexplained phenomena such as:

- In 1980 Dr. Kenneth Ring a psychologist from the University of Connecticut proposed that near-death experiences could be explained by the holographic model. Ring, who is president of the International Association for Near-Death Studies, believes such experiences, as well as death itself, are really nothing more than the shifting of a person's consciousness from one level of the hologram of reality to another.

- In 1985 Dr. Stanislav Grof, chief of psychiatric research at the Maryland Psychiatric Research Center and an assistant professor of psychiatry at the Johns Hopkins University School of Medicine, published a book in which he concluded that existing neurophysiological models of the brain are inadequate and only a holographic model can explain such things as archetypal experiences, encounters with the collective unconscious, and other unusual phenomena experienced during altered states of consciousness.

- At the 1987 annual meeting of the Association for the Study of Dreams held in Washington, D.C., physicist Fred Alan Wolf delivered a talk in which he asserted that the holographic model explains lucid dreams (unusually vivid dreams in which the dreamer realizes he or she is awake). Wolf believes such dreams are actually visits to parallel realities, and the holographic model will ultimately allow us to develop a "physics of consciousness" which will enable us to begin to explore more fully these other-dimensional levels of existence.

- A 1987 book entitled *Synchronicity: The Bridge Between Matter and Mind*, Dr. F. David Peat, a physicist at Queen's University in Canada, asserted that synchronicities (coincidences that are so unusual and so psychologically meaningful they don't seem to be the result of chance alone) can be explained by the holographic model. Peat believes such coincidences are actually "flaws in the fabric of reality." They reveal that our thought processes are much more intimately connected to the physical world than has been hitherto suspected.

  So science is fast catching up with religion and mysticism and although all these experiences I had seem on the surface to be very diverse are in fact reflections of the one reality, of course, how could it be any other way?

My personal belief is that the mystics of old may also have known all of this and is why they teach a practise of good and right living, because we affect more than we realise and they knew the importance of living in harmony with the environment. The devotional practices of prayer and meditation can help raise the awareness and consciousness of the practisers to touch the higher realities / dimensions and help to take humans to the next level of evolution, which I believe is the spiritual evolution of man, but that does not mean everyone has to believe in a God, only in the ability of humankind to rise above their present state to a higher level of being. One which makes us more compassionate towards others and have a love of all things in nature and humanity in its diversity, and reach the ability and desire to be in harmony with all people and the environment in which we share. As certainly unless we stop raping the environment and stop our tribe like ways of warring with each other we will surely not survive.

I hope that this was as interesting a journey for the reader as it was for me and has given some inspiration for further personal investigation and discoveries. I hope that you will go out and take pictures and videos of all the anomalous phenomena that you find and share it with the rest of us by posting on the internet and writing about it. Treat others as you would expect yourself to be treated and encourage love and understanding. It is easy to find the differences between each other and point to them rather than find the similarities and share those instead.

24.Further reading

Michael Talbot : The Holographic Universe ISBN-10: 0586091718 ISBN-13: 978-0586091715

UFO's

John A. Keel : UFOs – Operation Trojan Horse ISBN-10: 0349120854 ISBN-13: 978-0349120850

http://www.timothygood.co.uk

Timothy Good: Above Top Secret: Worldwide UFO Cover-up

ISBN-10: 0586203613 ISBN-13: 978-0586203613

http://www.nickredfern.com

Nick Redfern: On the Trail of the Saucer Spies: UFOs and Government Surveillance ISBN-10: 1933665106 ISBN-13: 978-1933665108

Nick Redfern: Three Men Seeking Monsters: Six Weeks in Pursuit of Werewolves, Lake Monsters, Giant Cats, Ghostly Devil Dogs and Ape-men ISBN-10: 0743482549 ISBN-13: 978-0743482547

http://en.wikipedia.org/wiki/Rendlesham_Forest_Incident

Georgina Bruni: Rendlesham incident: You Can't Tell the People: The Definitive Account of the Rendlesham Forest UFO Mystery ISBN-10: 033039021X ISBN-13: 978-0330390217

http://www.ufos-aliens.co.uk

M.I.B's (Men in Black)

http://en.wikipedia.org/wiki/Men_in_Black

http://www.ufos-aliens.co.uk/cosmicmib.htm

Ouspensky and The Fourth Way

http://en.wikipedia.org/wiki/Fourth_Way_%28book%29

http://www.fourthwayteaching.org/

P.D. Ouspensky: The Fourth Way: Teachings of G.I. Gurdjieff ISBN-10: 0140190228 ISBN-13: 978-0140190229

P.D.Ouspensky: Tertium Organum (1922) ISBN-10: 1594622051 ISBN-13: 978-1594622052

On telepathy and remote viewing: Ingo Swann-Penetration

http://en.wikipedia.org/wiki/Ingo_Swann

Ingo Swann: Penetration: The Question of Extraterrestrial and Human Telepathy ISBN-10: 0966767403 ISBN-13: 978-0966767407

Buddhism

Good introduction to Buddhist teachings for the serious :

Walpola Rahula: What the Buddha Taught ISBN-10: 0802130313 ISBN-13: 978-0802130310

The Pali cannon Online:

http://www.accesstoinsight.org/tipitaka/

http://www.palicanon.org/

http://www.leighb.com/studygid.htm

Devas: http://en.wikipedia.org/wiki/Deva_%28Buddhism%29

Printed in Great Britain
by Amazon

46365545R00078